GW01311936

Contents

Introduction

What you're about to read is my personal adventure through the seduction community. A few years ago I had hit this point in my life where I was having no success with women and knew something had to be done about it. I had read some books and searched the Internet, which lead me to this. It all started with one post on an Internet forum on the 5th of July 2006. This forum is where guys discussed women and seduction.

This is the journey I took through my first year in the pick up community. Here are my success stories, failures, realizations and insights into how I developed a lot of my theories.

My First Post: July 05, 2006

Hey Guys,

Thanks for welcoming me. It was a seriously good night and a definite eye opener for a newbie like me.

Adam

Unknown to me at the time this was the first of what would be many, many posts on that forum, each one bringing me one step closer to my goal of being able to reach my personal holy grail: the perfect woman.

The forum was, and probably still is, populated with hundreds of guys looking to achieve their own personal goals, all revolving around the same single topic – women. Whether they wanted to lose their virginity, sleep with hundreds of girls before they reached the age of 25, find their perfect girlfriend or learn how to sleep with a stripper, this was the place to come.

It was a haven for men with no understanding of the secretive creatures we know as women. It was a place where they discuss and teach each other the things they felt their parents should have taught them.

I only had a simple goal. I wanted to meet the perfect girl, the girl of my dreams. Someone who a *Dungeons and Dragons* role playing geek could only ever fantasize about. I wanted a tall, slim, sexy, down to earth, funny, popular girl. The kind of girl who would have made prom queen at school. The kind of girl who would probably have been nice enough to not push me down the stairs at school, and may even have shot the odd smile to the awkward, nerdy school kid. The kind of girl who was the head cheerleader in those high school movies you watch whilst growing up.

In real life I doubt that many geeks end up dating that prom queen. Were I not so much of a geek, maybe I'd have had a chance. Unfortunately for me, I was that geek.

I'd love to say I wasn't the stereotypical geek at school, but unfortunately I was. From my gel slicked hair and side parting with a small clump at the front that refused to go down no matter how much gloop you put on it, through to my awkward walk and hunched over body posture from carrying a bag too heavily filled with all of my school books for every day of the week and acne ridden face with wonky teeth. I was pretty much as stereotypical as you could get.

I remember crying after I left school. Not with tears of sadness, nor even with tears of joy, but with tears of regret – regretting all of the things I'd never done, and all the girls I didn't kiss. I decided at the age of 15 I'd do something about it. Though unfortunately for me it took me 10 years to do something serious about it.

A friend of mine told me about Neil Strauss's book *The Game* while I was in a particularly damaging relationship. Unfortunately it took another six months, hundreds of massive arguments, a break up and the loss of property worth over £2,000 to finally make me read it. He told me that I'd take to it like a duck to water. I read it within a day.

Note: The writings in this book were originally intended for an online forum. Since then the stories have been taken and collected to make this diary. We have kept the text in its original form so any spelling errors or typos were left to preserve the authenticity.

The Beginning

Watching those guys on that first day I went out with them was incredible. They were opening random girls, people they had never met. Although they didn't get every girl's phone number, they got more than I could ever imagine getting myself.

There was one girl in particular that caught my eye: a hot blonde standing alone by the side of a small ice-cream shop. Everyone had approached her and failed. I decided it would be good for me to try.

I don't remember exactly what I said, but I did manage to get her phone number. Not a great deal in the scheme of things, she never replied to my texts and didn't recognize me when I stopped her in the streets again a few weeks later. But it was witnessed by everyone around me, who were very impressed at my game. Nothing big yet, but I had been noticed.

I went home feeling good.

For the first time in a long time, I had learnt a valuable lesson. You CAN meet a girl randomly on the street and get her to like you. Maybe, just maybe, there was a hope for the geek yet.

I had a flat mate who completely disagreed with what I was doing. He would often ridicule me as I dived out to go practicing in Leicester Square. This was all to change when his girlfriend dumped him. I decided to make things better by taking him out to a strip club for the night...

The Stringfellows Disaster: July 06, 2006

I went out sarging for the first time on Tuesday and thought I did OK by getting a number close on my first HB7.5. So after that I decided I would go along to Stringfellows just to try my hand at stripper game. Knowing I would fail, what did I have to lose? ...

Little did I know.

I didn't have a wing, so I called my flat mate and invited him to come with me. I explained a few of the basics. Knowing I would fail there didn't seem to be much point going into detail.

We stand by the bar and a stripper approaches. She was nothing amazing looks-wise but still, she touches my arm and I use a quick "hands off the merchandise" routine. I turn this into a "sexual predator" routine, discussed with my friend, and the girl gets quickly into the conversation. In fact, she gets really into it and invites two more girls to defend all females honour to justify the fact that they are not all predators. This was ten minutes into a three way conversation and little did I know how terrible this would turn.

My friend gives me a 'wow man I can't believe this shit works' look and then starts giving massive indicators of interest to the first girl. At this the conversation shifts drastically. The other girls walk off, and him and her are getting close... but it's on her terms. The next thing I know I turn around and my friend and the girl are gone.

About 45 minutes pass and I see the stripper without my friend. "What have you done to my friend?" I asked.

She tells me he has gone to get money to pay for his dance. I start to suspect that bringing my friend may not have been such a good idea.

Thirty minutes later and she approaches with a big man in tow. "Where's your friend?"

"I have no idea, has he paid you?"

Obviously he hasn't paid and now it is becoming increasingly obvious he has left me to fend for myself.

Naturally, I offer to reimburse the girl the £20 for the dance only to be told that my friend didn't just dance with her. He danced with two girls and took added extras (whatever that means)! He owes them around £120. I give them the £20 for good will and say that I won't pay for my friend but I will look for him and get him to pay them back.

When I finally find my friend, I find out the poor sap actually thought the technique had worked so well that he had pulled! He accepted everything the girls offered, and then when it was time to pay, he made an excuse and ran for the hills! He actually ended up in East Putney through fear of being chased.

All in all not a great success.

Still, I wouldn't let that stop me. I continued my routine of daily sarging, working until 9pm and then out on the streets until 2am every single day. I'd decided to meet up with one of the gurus, Catnap.

Meeting Catnap: July 06, 2006

So today I met up with Catnap for a coffee and a chat in central London.

While sitting there, who do we see but Kellie Shirley and Kara Tointon better known as Carly Wicks and Dawn Miller from *Eastenders*.

I'm sitting there with a girl of my own who suddenly looks up and says "OMG, it's those girls from *Eastenders!*"

Catnap has absolutely no idea who they are... but after both me and my HB8 convince him they are celebrities, he moves in.

They are standing just outside the door. He approaches at the correct angle and comments on how nice Kara Tointon's belt is. He asks where she got it from, she says she doesn't remember but smiles and said that it was ordered in. He comments that the two buttons on the front are cute and wonders if thats part of her

Bat Utility Belt to call her Batmobile. She laughs and turns to face him. He asks if they are looking for a seat and that they may like to join us.

The girls mention that they are just waiting for one of their sisters to arrive otherwise they would. Catnap returns to sit with us. Then the girls meet the sister and Kellie's boyfriend. They split up and go on their separate ways. Kara then moves directly in front of Catnap, turns, waves, says goodbye (an indicator of interest), and then gives proximity by standing close to him. The sister appears to be in some form of rush so they don't stand around long enough to make a move.

They then head back to Starbucks for a brief second before moving off again past Catnap and giving one more acknowledgement and indicator of interest.

Catnap was the man. The sister was definitely a tough girl, and I couldn't help but feel I should have helped him out more as a wing. Unfortunately I was occupied with the HB8 and a bit nervous since I'm new to this.

Catnap's original approach definitely opened up Kara and caused a few IOI's.

Catnap's summary to me was - Celebrities are easy to chat to if you don't know who they are.

By now you may be wondering where the girl came from. Well, I decided to post up that field report soon after. I'd learnt some of the lingo and now referred to girls as HB's (hot babes) and indications of interest as IOI's. I was becoming more and more involved in the game.

Sound Republic: July 07, 2006,

Sound Republic on a Monday night has become a bit of a regular for me. I don't know what it is about that place, there just seems to be a high ratio of girls to guys.

Ok so I'm in the club and I see a gorgeous four set walk down some stairs. They were three oriental HB8's and their friend.

I have a personal problem approaching HB's I really like, and one of the Oriental's was most definitely my type, half white and half Filipino.

Anyway after about an hour or so, they sat on a couch quite close to me and I knew it was now or never. They were trying to take a picture of themselves, so I stepped up and offered to do it for them.

After the photo I sat with them so we could all look at the shot, and then commented, "I'm disgusted." They looked at me in shock.

"Four gorgeous girls and not one drink between them. Ok girls, this round is on me." Then I point to the HB8 I really like and tell her to come with me and tell me what everyone likes. I tuck her under my arm (she is only 5'1") and move to the bar.

She is very comfortable standing close to me. I give her a little kino which she returns and then we spend the night on the couch together with her body against me. I number close and k-close, and we arrange to meet again.

This was the HB8 I had on my lap when I had coffee with Catnap. It did cost me a round of drinks, but since then she pays her way. I'll post up any progression.

Adam

...

A lot of people queried my payment of the drinks. I responded with this:

...

That's a really interesting question.

I mean, I suppose I often buy a first drink. HB8 is a student, and I often buy students a drink with the phrase that their money is no good for me, as most places won't take monopoly money. Then they start to qualify themselves, and it enables me to get them to buy the next round.

I think as long as you open first without offering to buy the drink it can give you demonstration of higher value. Taking her to the bar to help choose the drinks also enabled me to isolate her and build rapport. Round of drinks cost me £13.

Last night we ended up in bed together.

I wasn't the only one putting posts up, and occasionally there were topics I felt I could help out with. When one person was looking for help connecting on a deeper level I thought I'd share my experiences.

Re: Relationships: July 07, 2006

Most of my experiences before the forum were all long term relationships,

For the past ten years or so I have only been single for nine months tops. The longest of these relationships was three years, and most of the others were at least a year long.

Funny enough I joined this forum to distance myself from the deep connections I always feel and to stop hurting the girls and myself when we break up.

The advice I would offer is to not dabble with deeper connections.

If it is meant to be it will happen naturally. It will happen as you spend more time together, exclusively. It will happen as you can relate to joint experiences together, and as you overcome hardships together. You will begin to wonder how you could deal with a situation alone, when you have always had her there at your side, and vice versa. If you really want to initiate it, go on holiday together. It will give you an insight into sharing your life with someone.

Be warned though, with a deeper connection comes pain. *Grief is the price we pay for love.*

Adam

Yet still my practicing continued, though by now I was hitting sticking points that I really needed help with. I was far from understanding the complicated mind of the female.

Learning: July 08, 2006

Last night I was invited out by an HB7 I used to know about a year ago. We had been in touch on and off and seeing as how she introduced me to one of my ex's, an HB8, I thought it could be an easy way to get into a pretty decent set.

I turn up with my friend, the Nigerian one from Stringfellows (I still don't have a real wingman). My HB friend hadn't arrived yet however she had booked a table, so we asked a barmaid where her table was and moved towards it. Sitting alone on the table was an absolutely stunning HB9.

I move over and introduce my mate and myself and explained how I knew the group. We start talking about common ground, such as our joint friend and I threw a few negs at her - "loner with no friends", "looks so young like a little kid." I saw no need for routines as I had an "in" already. Conversation is moving along pretty well when her HB8 sister turns up. I told her sister that HB9 was hitting on me and I'm glad she could come and save us.

I'm OK with using on-the-fly routines, so I asked their opinion on my Nigerian mate and his break up with his ex. "Was it cheating that she kissed another guy while on holiday?" My Nigerian mate once again missed the point of what was happening despite having been told about routines and launched into his entire life story with his ex. He then tried to neg me. I managed to divert his neg with humour, and was back chatting to HB8 about HB9.

Meanwhile my friend HB7 turns up with HB6 and another HB7. Then it turns to shit.

She introduces everyone at the table. When she gets to me she says, "This is AdamLondon. I know him because he went out with a friend of mine, then cheated on her with a few other girls before dumping her and leaving me to pick up the pieces. He is a nasty piece of work, and a user of women."

I didn't know what to do. All the HB's instantly changed their attitude towards me from open to hostile. Even my Nigerian friend looked shocked at what had been said. I knew I had to do something. I stammered something about being unfairly picked on, but it really didn't help. A very awkward moment passed when I came up with an idea. I move to HB9 and say, "You know, she's got me wrong. I'm not that terrible, I just like women. Besides I bet you aren't such a goody two-shoes."

It opened her up again. We start discussing it and she even asks about my past history. She loves the bad boy thing and is now giving me plenty of IOI's and a bit of kino. Time passes and I ignore her slightly in favour of opening up my HB7 friend whom I place a bet with that my ex would have stuck up for me over her damning tirade (ex is now a very good friend with benefits). We then phoned my ex and told her to tell HB7 she would stick up for me. I won £50

HB9 had gone over to the bar. I moved over next to her, gave her closed language and she opened conversation. She had already ordered herself a drink, I added mine onto the bill and told her I would let her buy me a drink.

We chat a little more, and she mentions a friend of hers would love me, some guy into video games or something. So I say, "Give me your number and we can all arrange to hook up." Number close.

We then move back to our table, which is now full so I mention we get our own seats somewhere else to continue our conversation in private. I steer the conversation towards sex by using the game *Marry, Fuck, Kill.* Then we both discuss sexual partners. It turns out that this girl has only had sex once in her life, as she only sleeps with guys she really has deep feelings for. I think on this for a while and then decide that

Morals + Effort = Can't Be Bothered. Plus, she told me that in bed all she does is lie on her back and let the guy do all the work. Not my kind of girl, unless this was a shit test...any views?

At about this point I realised it was customary for people to share their contacts, especially with regards to accessing clubs with hot girls. I thought I should aid as best I could.

Guestlists: July 19, 2006

Hi Guys,

I work as a Public Relations Manager in the video games industry. This Friday a contact of mine is running a party at Umbaba, the nightclub in Carnaby Street. This club is usually members only, and on this particular night it is invitation only. As the guy running the event is a friend of mine he has given me a guestlist. Now I have already invited a whole bunch of girls that I know as social proof, and was wondering if anyone from the forum wanted to come along and try sarging at what should be quite a decent profile event.

It is a 21 and over venue.

I can get a number of girls in free, so first come first served. It may make a good night to drag a girl out on a day2 to a high profile club.

Be warned, entry to the club is £20 a head and you have to be on the guestlist. If anyone wants to come along feel free to private message me.

I need the full names of anyone that wants to come by Thursday night.

All the best,

AdamLondon

I'd started getting a bit more involved in the community and referred to myself as "AdamLondon". I didn't want an abstract alias but still didn't want to get recognized by any girl who may accidentally stumble upon my posts. Adam from London became AdamLondon.

This party gave me a great excuse to talk to girls...though I wouldn't realise how powerful this could become just yet.

Practicing: July 21, 2006

I see a pair of girls handing out a sports magazine at Bond Street Station on my way to work this morning. I decide they both look OK. Probably borderline HB6.5 -7 and I figure good chance to practice sarging.

I take a leaflet, look over it and then hand it back saying, "Hmm you should give out two at once, that way you'd get rid of them sooner."

I exchange a bit of banter, then look at the other girl to notice she is giving IOI's. I swop girls saying, "So how many have you got left to hand out?"

Then ask, "What do you do for fun? You should come out to a party." Then I tell her about the event I have going on tonight. She apologises and says she is working and can't make it, so I ask for her email to let her know of other parties, then pull out my phone and say, "Doh wrong phone...my email phone is at home. Give me your number instead."

So I number close her and say I'd best get to work. Two hours into the day I text her. We trade a few texts, and now she has invited me out next Saturday with her and her friends to a club they are going to.

I can't be sure if it was technique so much as having the guts to talk to them in the first place.

As you can tell from the previous post I was itching to spread my wings and develop some ideas of my own. I didn't want to use the same routines everyone else did. I wanted to find things that fitted to my personality. I posted my first pieces of advice up.

Fun things to try out. 1 of 3 - The Complimentary Tap Water Technique: July 23, 2006

Hi Guys,

I just spent the weekend hanging out with everyone form the recent bootcamp. It was an absolute laugh, a quick hi to everyone that attended. Anyway, while out I came up with a few ideas that I thought you guys might like to try. There were three in total. So I thought I'd write each one up individually for you to read.

The first is the Complimentary Tap Water technique.

Two PUA's and myself were sitting in a well known ice cream cafe in Leicester Square when I noticed two HB's and a guy sitting at a table opposite. Then I hit on this idea. I ordered them three glasses of complimentary tap water and had them sent over.

Now initially the waitress didn't want to do it. We had to get her to bring us the glasses and then get someone else to take them over. When the girls received the drinks they were told who had provided the drinks.

We were looking at them with peacock sunglasses, raised the lenses and gave them a cheesy wink.

We only tested it the one time but I have to admit it was a great laugh and received a load of IOI's, not to mention a cheap way of buying a girl a drink.

Why not give it a try? It'd be good to hear of anyone else's successes or failures.

AdamLondon

Fun things to try out 2 of 3 - The Magic Bean Opener: July 23, 2006

We used this quite a few times, it actually opens a set really well. It gives you a constant point to return back to and really makes the target laugh if done correctly.

You take a handful of coffee beans from your local Starbucks. Then open sets asking if they want to trade something for your magic beans. Press on by telling them about how they will grow into a beanstalk and lead the person to a land in the clouds where they can get golden goose eggs. Say, "Come on that has to be worth some kind of trade?"

I did get a number close out of this one, and if done correctly it is easy to change thread.

AdamLondon

Fun things to try out 3 of 3 - Trouser Belt Limbo: July 23, 2006

Ok guys, final technique.

In my honest opinion, this is gold dust. It helped me number close an HB9 and an HB8 last Friday night. I noticed a bunch of girls in On Anon a few weeks ago standing in front of the bar getting people to limbo under the belt if they wanted to get past.

So on Friday at Umbaba I decided to give it a go. I took my belt off, gave one end to an HB9 pivot of mine, then all my friends started limboing underneath in time to the music. This attracts A LOT, I repeat A LOT, of IOI's from nearby girls. Then a simple hand gesture will hook the girls into playing Limbo with you. This really works.

I had been trying to hook the HB9 all night to no avail; she literally ignored all my opens. However one gesture from the Trouser Belt Limbo and she was hooked.

A word of warning, the bar staff did not like it at all and told us to stop the game. However that gave me the chance to talk to the HB9 and number close her.

Anyway guys, I hope you have fun with these. While writing this, the HB8 just called and asked me to Day 2 her right now. So I'm off.

Let me know how you get on with these.

AdamLondon

The latest one of these I still use to this day. It is amazing at generating Social Proof. In fact it worked so well...I had some follow up posts to write.

Limbo: July 24, 2006

Dude that night was off the hook!

We used the Limbo routine I mentioned in another thread to open up a bunch of other sets and I number closed an HB8.5. I did Day 2 the Filipino girl last night. Didn't f-close but did get her to commit to coming over mine to repeat the lap dance this Friday.

If you have strong inner game the girl will recognise it. She will be attracted to the Alpha Male within!!!

An Alpha male doesn't need to show he is the man, because he knows it.

AdamLondon

The Filipino girl became a bit of a personal battle for me, and represented an unobtainable target...one of the achievements I so wanted...so naturally I wrote a post.

This girl has, by her own admission, 20 Lets Just Be Friends guys... on: July 24, 2006

Ok guys, I've had a few people ask me how it went on with the HB 8.5 I pulled at Umbaba last Friday. I thought I'd write it here for you all to take a look at.

Background: I managed to get this chick to give me a lap dance whilst at Umbaba. I mentioned kissing and she says, "I suppose you want to kiss me." I said "Please, I don't kiss girls I have just met. I don't know what lurgees I may catch." I used a lot of push-pull during the night and also had to freeze her out twice in response to comments about how we are just friends, dancing and having fun. I number close by telling her I'll get her email sometime later and send her copies of the photos I took of us.

The next day I receive a text. “Adam! How’s Eve? Has she finally let you taste her sinful, sweet, juicy flesh? How are you? Can u email me last nights pics if you can?”

I do the only thing to be done. I ignore her. The next day I look at my phone after the bootcamp and notice that I have a missed call from her. I call her back

Adam: Hey girl... you left me a missed call?

Girl: Yes I did

Adam: ...

Girl: ...

Adam: Ok, why?

She explains that she is planning on going out with her friend on a date to back them up. I point out this makes her a third wheel and a loser and said she should get company. She asks if I am inviting myself. I say, “OMG, no. I’m tired and am off to bed. You can find some other chump to keep you company.” I then relent and say, “Look being a third wheel sucks. If you get bored call me. If I’m around I may turn up.”

Later on I get two more missed calls. What can I say? I don’t like answering my phone. I call back... “What do you want?”

It turns out she decided to let her friend go alone and now she is thinking of going out to dinner. I point out she is still a sad loner but I will accompany her so she doesn’t look too bad.

We go out to dinner. I only have a small bite to eat so naturally she pays. Then I offer to walk her home to save her from weirdos. Not for her but for me because if something happens to her I will feel guilty and I don’t need that right now... I’m busy at work.

We get to her place and sit outside her flat. There is some serious push-pull going on now from both of us. She freezes me out and I match her freeze position to build rapport. Then change position so that it breaks her freeze. This was a real battle of wills.

It was only when we moved into her reception that the conversation changed and I truly realised what I was up against. The girl is a singer, in a band that is very close to being launched. She has done a good number of gigs, and is due to do a few more. Her day jobs also bring in over £35K a year.

I then realised that she was being difficult and having so many bitch shields not because she looked like a 9.5 - 10 but because she believed herself to hold that kind of value. So I had more shit to go through.

Anyway, she sang me some songs. I told her that when she sang she really came alive, like I could see her true self. Before that I said I thought she was a little fake and boring. Then I sang along with her. I'm not a great singer but can hold my own and had a little training as a kid. She said she was impressed and we did a few duets. I played it down telling her I was crap but just sang because I loved doing it. Then I said it was time for her bedtime. I really wanted to get this in before her because I felt she would say it soon. She pointed out that I should go because I have work in the morning. I told her that as I am the head of the department I can take the morning off, she doesn't have that kind of excuse and will get fired. DHV.

Finally I walk to the door. We are hugging now and we break embrace. I turn once more at the door, we share a massive hug and I move in for the kiss. She turns it into a hug. I freeze her out and leave saying bye.

So I'm walking down the road cursing myself for my shit escalation. Then I figure I'll write a negging text.

"Hey girl, I can't believe I actually enjoyed myself tonight. I really thought you were just a shallow bitch that..."

My phone rings, it's her. "Remember to send me the pictures!"

I then tell her she can keep me company as I walk home. So we talk. Conversation moves back onto the lap dance. I tell her it was pretty good. She says she can do better, but didn't want to get me hard. I tell her that no girl can get me hard with just some shitty dance. I need emotional contact and a matching rapport and personality. She says that she can do it. I tell her I accept the challenge.

Anyway, this Friday night at 11 p.m. at my house the challenge is on. Me, armed with my own will power, and whatever self control I have over my penis.

Her with a freaky dancing body, and Britney Spears *I'm a Slave 4 U.*

Round 3. Guys It's on!

People grew more and more curious about my personal battles, so I elaborated.

Personal Battles: July 24, 2006

She has soo many shit tests I feel like I'm studying for a degree in fertilisation. I also feel if I don't handle it just right I'll end up being LJBF. She really DHV's herself though, which is why I think that despite her looks she feels that she is a 9 or a 10.

She has been texting me steady all day, and I'm making her wait a good few hours between each text. Although she has been doing it to me as well. It's almost like sarging a bloody PUA!!!

Anyway I'll keep you posted about Day 3.

AdamLondon

Developing into a PUA

Within only a month and a half I was getting some serious results. I was working with a small seduction company based in London and this routine would end up getting me a small bit of notoriety. That notoriety was based on a video of me using it to get a kiss within one minute of meeting a girl in the street!

The Marriage Opener/Close on: July 26, 2006

Ok guys.

This one is amazing. It was originally developed by James DeMarco and then refined by Mr. DeMarco, Tomcat and myself. This routine should allow you to open and get a number close within two minutes.

When we warmed up we got a 100% success rate on about six sets, one after the other. You need a strong wing for this to work.

Approach a set.

"OMG, OMG, OMG, There is something I have to ask you."

Drop to one knee.

"Will you marry me?" Hold out a cheesy ring.

Wing dives in at this point... "OMG, I'm a priest! Let me conduct the wedding."

Wing grabs all of the obstacles/cock blocks and pulls them away. "You can all be witnesses"

Then grab your target by the arm, and place it in yours. (Kino)

The Priest begins the ceremony.

"Do you AFC Adam take this... What's your name? ..."

AFC Adam says, “I do.”

Then he asks the girl the same thing. Don’t wait for a response. The wing cuts in with you may now kiss the bride.

Extend your cheek for her to kiss. I tried turning my head last minute for a lip kiss and this does work if you feel like you wanna go for it. Then priest takes a photo of you both kissing.

Then turn to your wife, chat a bit of rubbish about how fun that was, maybe hug a bit. Then ask if she wants you to text the photo to her? If she says no say, “OMG, come on, these are our wedding photos!”

Then simply collect the number!

AdamLondon

Marriage Opener Field Report: July 27, 2006

As I mentioned above, the routine gave me the following field report.

Ok I am still reeling after my sarging session with James Demarco and Tomcat last night. These guys are off the hook!

Catnap was kind enough to introduce me to James and Tomcat. These guys took me under their wing and have been training me solid, for like the last 3 weeks in exchange for some work I am doing for them.

Last night was the most incredible experience ever.

We were out testing their new Marriage Opener/Close. Now I have to point out here, it isn’t about asking someone to marry you. There is a definite psychology going on behind the whole routine and this stuff is powerful! This is the second time I have seen them use this routine. After a few warm up sets once more we had 100% success on number closes!

I knew this thing got number closes but last night I got my first one minute kiss close! I literally didn't even know her name before we had our tongues down each other's throats! What makes this even better is the fact that my mate filmed the entire thing on his phone!

This set was so hostile initially even telling us that they had partners. I have never experienced anything like this before.

Guys, I owe you all soo much. Man I love this community!

AFC AdamLondon

This was the first time I would sign off as AFC AdamLondon, the name I would adopt from this point forward. It was a sign of my acknowledgement that I was a student and always looking for better ways to improve myself.

Social Proof was becoming something I was more and more familiar with, and I'd learnt to generate it cold.

FR Tiger Tiger HB7.5 aka Frenchie on: August 02, 2006, 07:14:38 PM

I am fortunate enough to be having Crazy Serb and Spike to be crashing at my place during their time in the UK. They arrived last night at about 10 p.m.

Naturally they wanted to go straight out and sarge. It was an amazing experience. Me and Colonel got to go out with Beckster and his wing, Crazy Serb and Spike, and finally Tomcat and James DeMarco. What a team. Unfortunately Tomcat and James had to dive off early as they had a lot of work to get done with the seminar today and their other bits.

Still, watching a group of four MPUA's was amazing. We had social proof within about 25 minutes. Most of the sets were giving IOI's.

One 2-set were dancing quite well on the floor. Beckster had number closed them already but I don't think they were his type (neither was blonde).

I moved in and danced with them and played a nice game of sticking my hand in front of one of the girl's faces in a "talk to the hand" kind of way. This really pissed her off and prompted her to swear at me with her middle finger.

This then turned into us trading rude gestures towards one another until I spotted one she used from the TV show Friends. I then duplicated it with another one I saw from the show. You could almost see it read across her face... Rapport!

The next thing you know I isolate her by the bar and we share a very sexually charged dance. I speak to her this time with the little French I know. Once again, you can see it... Rapport!

I love escalating a girl's buying temperature. By now she was almost rubbing her lips across my neck. I lean in for the kiss and presto! K-close. After the kiss I ask for her name and get her number.

Today I day2 her for one hour at Starbucks. Actually, I had social proof again and it is probably my favourite way of generating attraction. I had managed to open about three sets outside Starbucks in Leicester Square, starting with a guy and 2 HB5's then incorporating a pair of HB8.5's and a young couple. By the time Frenchie turned up I was centre of attention and was tucking into a free Krispy Kreme doughnut I blagged off of a girl walking by.

I isolate her inside, and instantly start generating kino. It takes about two minutes to regenerate the kiss and then get her to place my hands in her lap. We talk about movies and favorite genres. I told her my favorite movie is Le Bossu a French flick. She mentions she hasn't seen it and so now this Friday night she is coming over to watch it with me... I'll keep you posted.

Now I was really seeing a difference in my game, though I was still nowhere near able to catch my perfect girl, at least not

comfortably. Now I didn't just want the perfect girl, I wanted to be able to make it really special. I wanted her to know that no matter who else would ever talk to me I would only want her. I wanted her to know that I could have had almost anybody else but I'd chosen her.

I was going to have to practice. Practice a lot. Then I got my first crack at a true 10 out of 10.

The First 10: August 04, 2006

OK guys so I am waiting to get on the train at Finchley Road when I see this cute little HB8.

The train pulls into the station and I find myself waiting at the door with a pair of business type gents and the HB8. She gets flustered and moves to another door.

I decide best action would be to enter through the door I have already decided upon and approach inside. Then me and the two guys have a clash of chivalry, all bumping into each other trying to allow the other to go first. I joke with them both (social proof I tell myself), then I enter the train...

... As I am looking towards the HB8 my eyes are drawn to another girl. An HB10 sitting right in front of me. I make a quick no brainer decision, and sit with the two guys from outside and ignore the HB8. I notice she has a beautiful engraved crucifix around her neck leading to a pair of gorgeous breasts. I decide to open with...

"I guess a lot of guys stare at your breast while saying you have beautiful eyes. Well I'm different. I will stare into your eyes and tell you that you have beautiful breasts."

I then scrap that idea, and go with, "Is that a real crucifix or is it just a floral pattern conveniently disguised as a crucifix?"

(Blank Stare)

..."You see I'm looking to buy something for my sister, and I was wondering where you got that from."

She responds... In bloody French.. "Je Desole, Je parle Francais." Or something like that..

Thankfully I remember some of my French from school, and it has been recently revitalised thanks to Frenchie HB7.5. Who for some weird reason thinks it's sexy when I speak French to her... You'd think she gets enough of that from her home country.

Anyway, I respond (in very poor French, but with a sexy French accent.. ask Frenchie!) "No problem I can speak French, though only a little."

We then talk for a while, she compliments my French, I perve over her tits. I then ask her if she has been clubbing during her stay in the UK? She says that she hasn't, so I offer for her and her friends to join us tomorrow night. She agrees and we swop numbers.

We talk a little further, and I ask her where she is staying. "Harlesden" she replies. And then laughs...

In a true East London accent says "I'm sorry, I can't do it any more... I feel so bad. I'm from London, I just grew up in France as a kid."

It was a bloody bitch shield!

We both get off at the same station, sharing a little bit of kino. I tell her how no-one ever gets to wind me up and that she should count that as a victory. She asks about the club and says that we should go to the club she dances for.... Stringfellows.

I tell her perhaps another time, but it would be good to see her at the club.

I expect she won't turn up at the club, but I do plan on playing a bit of text game with her. We shall see what happens.

AFC AdamLondon

I was still dabbling with different ways to open sets, I hadn't stumbled on anything that seemed to consolidate what I was doing. There was something missing.

The L Shaped Hand Opener on: August 07, 2006

Ok guys, here's a quick one I developed over the weekend at the Tomcat/Demarco Bootcamp.

It's pretty simple and works really well on HB8's +.

Anytime you catch the eye of an HB point directly at her and make an L sign on your forehead in the "Loser" vein.

The response is amazing, she will spit out a whole bunch of IOI's at you. Most respond with a really big smile, others will actually approach you and say, "You don't even know me", or "Well so are you." Either way, if they speak to you they have opened you, and you can use it to generate attraction.

The only girl to give me a bad response from this out of about 30 or so I tested it on called me a wanker in return. I held my frame, accepted that I was but told her that doesn't stop her being a loser. Guess what happened... She re-opens me as I am leaving the club and gives me a massive hug and kiss on the cheek. She was only an HB5 and so I think the reason she responded so harshly was that it functioned as an overneg.

Still, it's a great way of opening a lot of people really quickly. Try it yourself and let me know how it goes.

AFC AdamLondon

The Tourist Opener/Close on: August 07, 2006

Here is a nice little variation of the marriage opener/close.

It's great for newbies. A whole bunch of guys at the bootcamp tested it at the weekend and I believe most of them closed with it. Now in fairness you will need pretty good text/email game or a venue change to escalate things with it as it is subtle. But it makes a great way for new guys to get into game and to start beating back AA without embarrassing yourself too much.

Open a set with your wing and ask them to take your picture together. You both pose for the photo. Feel free to ask them if they know how to use a camera (Neg).

Once the picture is taken, you move into the set and look at the picture with the girl that took the photo. (Kino)

Your wing then takes the camera off you and suggests taking your picture with the target. This takes good frame control to pull off but is easy once you get the hang of it.

Finally you show the girl the photo and tell her that you will send her a copy. Then collect her email off her, and if you have the right kind of frame, control the phone number as well. You can tell her that you will send it via MMS, or just tell her to put the number down.

Give it a try, especially if you haven't had the chance to go out and sarge yet, or are just getting into the game.

AFC AdamLondon

I was beginning to receive direct questions asking me for help with specific sticking points people had.

Though I had only been in the game a short while, the practice I was getting really enabled me to improve at a rapid rate. Unfortunately the same couldn't be said for my job. Soon after writing this following post I was asked to resign, due to a lack of interest in the role. I was spending up to three hours a day on the phone to other PUA's.

How Can I Demonstrate Higher Value: August 13, 2006, 10:03:08 AM

There are a lot of ways we can try to demonstrate higher value without bragging. I think I'd start by saying something like. "Aww, man its a long story, maybe I'll tell you another time."

I find this is usually enough to spark their interest and get them to probe further.

So they are already a) buying into you, and b) committing to listen to you for a while.

Then I would create a story. I would highly recommend that this story is loosely based on an event in your life. Our own life experiences really make the best stories, as we have real facts to pull from. In our mind these memories are more colourful. We can add details like what the weather was like at the time and random things that other people might say that are often not included in made up stories.

Think of an event where you were really lucky in front of your friends or family, a tournament or competition that you won, skill that you have, or something memorable you did. These all make for good stories. You can tell about your friends telling you that you were amazing but you feel like it is all down to luck. You just say, "No I'm just lucky"... and the name stuck.

It can be an event that took place where you were the only person to be picked out of the crowd, and all your best mates were jealous, and so started they calling you lucky.

I might even be tempted to go along the route of saying... "Aww man I can't tell you... I get embarrassed." This will really hook them in. I would probably try and change the topic of conversation, but let them probe.

Then eventually say "Ok ok, but if i tell you, you owe me..., you have to..., you must..." Get the commitment and then I'd go to make her laugh by saying "It's something my mum used to call me when my mates were around when I was younger, I swear she did it just to embarrass me... and now it's sorta stuck." (Notice past tense)

AFC AdamLondon

By now I was beginning to get regular results, and variants of the one minute k-close were becoming more and more regular occurrences. Though still I was finding it hard to explain what was really happening.

Though the in-field reports kept coming.

---

3 minute K-Close at the Church Nightclub on Sunday August 16, 2006

I have had many of the students from the last bootcamp asking me how I get speedy k-closes. I thought that rather than PM everyone separately I would write a detailed FR here. I will make it as detailed as I can and try to give some idea into my thought processes as I go through.

I am standing just on the edge of the dance floor strumming my air guitar asking random people if they would like to join my band.

I spot a blonde HB8 standing alone and observe her for a while. I notice that she doesn't appear to be fidgeting, which tells me she probably isn't waiting for somebody to arrive. She isn't leaning on the wall by the toilets, so she is unlikely to be waiting for someone to finish there. I take the decision that she has probably just moved away from the dance floor for a rest.

I approach backwards, still strumming my air guitar. I pull up besides her and ask, "Would you like to join my band?"

She says, "Nah I don't think so." Never put off, I strengthen my control on the frame.

"Go on, just for one song"

She joins in, we mirror each other. I tell her she is pretty good and ask her if she has played before. She tells me that she doesn't even know the song. I say, "Well that is impressive playing for someone who doesn't know the track."

I then ask her name. When she tells me I stop playing, tell her mine and shake her hand. I then turn that into a twirl, and a quick little rock and roll dance routine. I spin her around a few times, at arms length and then a little closer, before pulling off a move that leaves me with my arm around her waist and both of us fairly close to each other.

I ask her where she is from, speaking slowly and deeply into her ear. She tells me she is from the States and I say that is so cool and how I have always wanted to go there. I then shift the tempo and move her out to arms length again, a few more twirls and then repeat my earlier move to bring us close together again.

She asks where I am from. I tell her London, again speaking deeply into her ear only coming up to stare into her eyes, and move back again. I am squeezing her hand gently as we dance against each other. She tells me that she loves London and that she really wants to stay longer. I ask her how long she is here for and she says 3 more days.

I then pull her out to distance and with high energy say "OMG, there is so much to see, what have you done so far?" I then move in closely so she can whisper into my ear. She tells me some random things and I make sure to comment on each one, slowly stroking her back as I do so. She responds by squeezing mine.

After a while I move her out again, and we dance at distance.

A few more twirls and I repeat my move bringing her in again. I then move in to talk to her. I ask her if she believes in being spontaneous then move out to look into her eyes as she answers. She says yes.

I ask her if she ever does something on the spur of the moment just because it feels right. I repeat the looking into eyes thing. She says yes. This time as I move in to whisper something else I go past her lips... I can feel she wants to kiss me but she is hesitant. There isn't enough comfort.

I then whisper to her, "How many restaurants have you been to?" She tells me not many. I move out to distance staring into her eyes holding her hands, squeezing them, then in high energy I tell her "OMG, you have to eat at Busaba, it's my favourite Thai restaurant. I'll take you!" She says "Really?" I say "Yes, either tomorrow or the next day depending on meetings." (DHV)

I ask "How can I get in contact with you?" She responds that she has no phone here. I ask if she can check her email? She says "Yes"!

I email close. Then as I put my phone away I pull her close to me, this time I can see it in her eyes, they start to close slowly, as I move towards her again. This time I don't move to her ear... K-Close. And the option of a Day2.

I hope this helps guys.

PM me if you have any questions.

AFC AdamLondon,

....

So, still the better I got, the more I wanted to know why it worked and more importantly why did this have value to me? Did I really know what I was looking for? Or had my dream of the perfect girl been shattered in the beds of all the other girls?

Do you know why you sarge?: August 18, 2006

Here's something I have been pondering recently.

Why do we sarge? Now I'm not talking collectively here, as obviously that would be to get girls. What I am referring to is our personal reasons for doing this, in short, what are your aims?

I have been going on a little mental journey, picking up girls and having fun yet have not really decided where my final aim is. It constantly feels that there is something missing. Something that was not missing when I was with my last girlfriend, during the good parts at least.

I think it is important that each of us understands what we are looking to get out of the community. Be it the perfect girl, a bunch of casual relationships or a relationship with a pair of lesbian strippers. Whether those goals change over time doesn't matter the point is that you set yourself a target and go for it.

Otherwise you could end up having sex with a number of different hot babes, yet still feel like something important is missing.

AFC AdamLondon

Yet still the reports kept coming in.

5min K-close at the Church on Sunday: August 21, 2006

Hi guys. I won't go into detail on this post as essentially I did exactly the same thing as last week to get the close.

The only difference this time is I convinced her to show me some snaps of her on her phone wearing lingerie. I didn't offer to do dinner this time as the vibe was much more sexual, although

I did have to increase comfort first by number closing and then saying we should meet for a coffee during the week.

A lot of the guys on the bootcamps have been asking the best way to k-close, and I still feel the strongest for me is the kiss on the cheeks routine and then lean in for the kiss. That way you can always just kiss the cheeks and maintain conversation, rather than being left with the awkward situation that follows the "would you like to kiss me?" and they say "No" scenario. Obviously you can turn that around, but I find a lot of people new to this would be put off by the initial rejection.

AFC AdamLondon

Around this time I began working on a very cute girl I had got chatting to from Denmark. She was a model out there, incredibly cute and really feisty. I'd been gaming her for a while and arranged to visit her. Unfortunately the original trip was cancelled, but I made a point of adding the MSN posts, I could to the forum.

MSN Conversation Denmark HB9: August 22, 2006

Ok guys, this is just to keep you informed of the long going saga with me and the HB9 from Denmark.

My flight got cancelled thanks to the terrorists so I can't see her until the 9th of Sept. Anyway, we just had an MSN conversation I thought I'd share with you guys. It kind of gives good insight into not reading too much into what a girl says, rather how she says it.

HB Denmark: You're cute

Adam: AHHHGHGHGHGHGH. NOOOO!!!!

Adam: I'm cute. Shit. That's it, it's all over.

HB Denmark: What?

Adam: I'm cute. I'm in the friend zone!

HB Denmark: I know, I know, guys hate girls calling them cute. LOL.

Adam: Because it means the end. No sex. No relationship. What follows is... the LJBF!!!!

Adam: The dreaded LJBF!!!!

HB Denmark: Oh Mr. Lyons, I can definitely tell you that you are NOT in the friend zone .

I don't know how helpful this is to you guys. I just thought I'd stick it up while I'm chatting to her.

AFC AdamLondon

Obviously I was still adding the odd bit of insight.

Some Insight: August 21, 2006

I have had a lot of success recently with this one at The Church in Kentish town, although I suspect it would work anywhere that plays similar music in the Australian American rock vein.

You just strum away on your air guitar to the music. As an HB approaches, ask her to join your band.

Instant Mirroring!

If you read my 3 min k-close FR you can see how I used it.

AFC AdamLondon

The Mirror, Rapport, Manouver Dance Floor Game routine: August 30, 2006

I just stuck this up on another site, but thought I'd copy it here for everyone to see.

This is my favourite routine to use on the dance floor. Tallbloke has seen this in action and Styx used it last night. I will let them tell you how much success can be had with it.

The premise is simple. You nudge a girl and tell her you like her dance moves and would she mind teaching you. You copy her moves, thus mirroring and generating rapport.

You then teach her something and continue for a while, chatting occasionally and dancing together.

Finally you maneuver her into your arms for a more sexual dance.

That's it, simple yet effective. Let me know how you get on.

AFC AdamLondon

The media at the time was very anti-game. It was something I really wanted to work towards fixing, and the community was very wary of dealing with any of them. The simple fact is most guys have no idea how to go about changing themselves. As always, the abusers got the media attention, which made things look bad for the users. Still I was determined to have a hand in changing those perceptions.

Re: Our Community Cast in a Negative Light...: August 31, 2006

I deal with the media on a regular basis.

There is an incredibly high chance that the negative media written was to slate the book [a seduction book published], purely to add a different opinion and thus gain interest in what he was writing. There is a lot of competition between the nationals to write different views from one another in order to generate interest and get people reading their pieces.

In fact I have been dealing very heavily with a premier national mens magazine recently for the School of Seduction. This should put the community in a very good light, but again I know this is only because they were looking to do a positive piece in the first place.

Unfortunately the media isn't the unbiased medium for news that we would wish it to be.

AFC AdamLondon

With the Filipino girl and the Danish girl who happened to be Vietnamese, not to mention a host of other Oriental and Asian girls, I was becoming a bit of a specialist.

So I decided to try and help others out who had the same tastes.

Asians, Orientals, and Other Family Value girls ... Oh My!: September 07, 2006

Those that know me well know that I really only go for cute little Oriental girls.

I have found that gaming them requires a few subtle changes in approach. These aren't massive but I have found that they can aid a lot. It should also be said that this is not a template that can be applied to all of them as individual backgrounds and parenting styles can affect this. However, I would say that for the traditional Oriental/Asian girl with strong family values these few tips have helped me close with pretty reliable results.

1) Don't go for the K-Close straight away.

They typically need a good amount of comfort, and are quite liable to suffer from buyers remorse if things move too fast. Number close, Day 2 at your house with a DVD then K-Close. If she is shy do not go for it in front of friends, hers or yours, unless she initiates it.

2) Talk about caring for your parents.

It is ingrained in their culture that they should look after their parents as they age. This is an area they expect most western people to fall down on. If you have this quality they will see you as different. I often get told "You're not like other western guys are you?"

3) Tell them you are bad, that you are naughty, the usual stuff... It works really well on them especially if you have portrayed yourself as a family kind of guy.

4) Learn their culture, even just a small amount.

Get them to teach you. The effort and time they spend in teaching you generates a lot of rapport, builds comfort and gives you a deposit.

4) Tell them you don't want a girlfriend as you are looking for "the one."

This last point is very very powerful and I expect it works on most girls.

I have recently begun telling girls I don't want a girlfriend until I meet the one I want to spend the rest of my life with. I then start qualifying them. They will often try and jump through hoops to be the one, but they accept you have a life outside of them and don't have an exclusive relationship. Therefore they don't wish to push the boundaries in case they mess up all the hard work they have put into being the one. I have had a lot of good results with this turning day 2's into FB's with pretty good results.

I hope this helps, If anyone has any other questions on this, feel free to PM me.

AFC AdamLondon

....

I was becoming infatuated with the model from Denmark and with the trip approaching I decided to drop a final thanks to the forum!

Off to Denmark! To meet my ideal HB? Thank you forum: September 09, 2006

Just wanted to drop a quick message into the forum before I leave.

The months I have spent here and all the skills I have learned I have been using on a model in Denmark. I have written a few FR's about how I have been gaming her over the phone and MSN. Anyway this is it, I'm finally off to go and meet her.

Last night she made me an offer of staying in her place instead of a hotel, as it would be a waste of money. So I know the f-close is there, but there are other things about this girl. We share a lot of similar interests (including Tekken)... so who knows.

So before I go I just wanted to say thank you to everyone on the forum for helping me and for all those who gave me pointers and advice on the way. This marks a significant point for me in my game, so I wanted to give a special thanks to Cryptic, James DeMarco, Beckster and of course Tomcat for really pushing my game. Of course, thanks to everyone else who has helped along the way, you guys know who you are.

See you all when I return!

AFC AdamLondon

As always even when abroad with a girl I really liked, I found time to post up my latest tips.

Can I Borrow Your Umbrella Opener + Hook: October 02, 2006

Hi Guys,

I was out sarging today with James Demarco and Tomcat, when it started pouring down with rain. We jumped at the chance to use this opener. Later today it occurred to me that I hadn't seen it on the forum yet.

Wait in a shop doorway until you see a decent one set with an umbrella.

Move over to her and say excuse me...

Make sure you stand outside of the umbrella getting wet and say, "I don't suppose you would mind if I borrowed your umbrella for a while, would you?" Then duck underneath it.

Before she has a chance to say no tell her you are only looking to travel a little way to complete your shopping. (Time constraint)

Then simply walk and talk. Simple yet effective.

Even rain doesn't stop day sarging.

AFC AdamLondon

Unfortunately the HB Denmark girl didn't hold my attention. It was amazing, I'd gone all the way out to meet her. She was beautiful, intelligent and a geek to boot. Yet something was missing. She wasn't the one; the chemistry just wasn't there.

I was about to make an astonishing discovery, one that would set me apart from a lot of the other PUA's in the world, I was about to understand the mentality of the HB9's and plus.

HB10's Umbaba FR: October 09, 2006

Hey Guys,

Sorry for not posting for a while, I've been a busy beaver.

Recently I have been trying to up my game and go for a different grade of HB. So it is with this in mind that on Saturday I find myself in Umbaba with Ninja and James1 going for a group of 8-9 HB10's.

Now I have to admit, in my opinion, these were probably not HB10's, but this brings me nicely onto my first point;

1) A group of girls will have their own perceived value.

If you have a group of guys in a club and only a few sets of HB5 girls and then an HB8 walks in she will see herself as the hottest girl in the club. Gaming her will now be a lot harder than usual. You will have to use techniques as if she was a 9 or 10.

So in Umbaba these girls thought of themselves as HB10's. To give you an idea they had all just come back from a fashion shoot in Milan, stopped off via Ibiza for 3 days partying, and then after one night back in London popped into Umbaba where they are all free members to celebrate one of the girls birthdays, before heading to Miss UKs after party bash at Cafe de Paris.

2) HB10's may not always have an UG or male to befriend to get into set.

Even if they have, these will usually have been approached in the past by naturals, so the HB's will know to stay away. I saw countless guys try to use me to get into set. Bad move. Everyone that tried got a polite comment and then I controlled them out of there.

Access to the set was hard. Their perceived value was very high, despite the fact I had completely sarged the room. I had already gained massive social proof, including access to a set of HB8+9 and a rich AMOG next to the set of 10's. You see, to the 10's social proof helped but didn't get me direct access, as they knew the owner of the club (and it wasn't me). Also, every other set isn't as attractive so they see the value as lower. They are also expecting to be approached. This means that the status you would normally get by having the guts to approach them isn't anywhere near as high, they really aren't as impressed as they would be on a day sarge. They know alcohol is giving people dutch courage to approach.

3) Social Proof via friends is ultimate power!

James DeMarco and Tomcat pointed this out to me afterwards as I analyzed the set. I gained access via one of the girls whom I befriended first. I went in under radar and LJBF'd her. I then asked for her advice on pulling women. This opened her up for a good 15 minutes, as we spoke about attraction and push pull etc, which is obviously a topic I could talk a lot about.

Once in the set with one of them, the girls completely opened up to me. Now at this point I cannot stress the value of a wing. Ninja was gaming one of the girls using dance game. Basically strutting his stuff with one of them, the girls asked if he was with me. After deciding we were both OK and together they accepted us into the group along with James1 who was social proofing the rest of the club like an animal.

From here it was pretty much plain sailing. The rest of the set was as you would expect. The best part was when the new girls joined the group... I was expecting a bunch of cock blocks to push us out. Instead I was given the warmest greeting! The girls we didn't even know greeted us with a kiss on the lips from each girl and a few slow dances. Both of the New Girls I number closed. I suspect the reason is that as they knew their friends had high value and if the other girls had accepted us into the group then we must have been OK or had enough DHV to warrant being nice to, on a first impression.

Social Proof with the rest of the club was amazing. The notable points were the HB9 that treated me like shit earlier in the night asking for a dance, the HB8 who kept trying to get into our pictures, and the countless IOI's from the HB7's as we left the club.

All in all a great night,

In summary.

1) Girls have perceived value, if there is only one 8 in the club game her like a 9

2) Large girl groups of hot babes may not have an UG to gain access, if not come in under the radar

3) Social Proof via friends, preferably theirs. If not, game an HB9/10 Pivot

4) BE CAREFUL WITH NEGS

Some girls, especially hot ones, will take a direct neg very badly. They will ask who are you to be insulting them. Very HOT girls have massive ego's, especially if they work in media. I didn't learn this from that night but from an off-the-cuff comment I made on another night. Start with gentle negs first and then up the damage as you get to know them better.

If you haven't had an HB10 girl before, go for one as a friend and get her to help you pull. It's easier than trying to lay her and will get you used to being around beautiful girls. The more comfortable you are the easier it will be to close them. Even if you don't get her, she will probably have a bunch of HB10 girl friends.

See you all soon!

AFC AdamLondon

The Arrival of the PUA

Shortly after this my game was going through the roof. I was closing almost every set I opened. I was growing fearful of my ability to close and afraid to let people know as most people simply refused to believe it. Yet I was closing almost 90% of the girls I spoke to.

I did receive an interesting phone call. My field reports were getting longer and more detailed. I was understanding what I was doing, just not able to structure it to others properly.

FR - Sports Cafe HB New York. Shit Tests: November 06, 2006

Hi guys,

I haven't written one of these for a while as I have kinda been up to my eyeballs with personal stuff. I thought I'd share one of my recent lay's as it gives a pretty good example of shit tests. This is post k-close.

I meet this girl in the Sports Cafe. The approach was easy, mostly down to eye contact and strong inner game. We talk for a while, dance for a while, talk for a while. I pull her in and k-close. Easy enough. We swap numbers and now the game begins.

As I mentioned I've been really busy for a while now, and really didn't have the time to day 2 her properly. So I took her out for a dinner and a coffee for about 1.5 hours. I told her I had a meeting straight afterwards. Dinner went well, I paid. Throughout I am using a lot of kino. I hold her under my arm, kiss her forehead when she tells a funny story and generally act as if she is my girlfriend.

I took her to Starbucks afterwards where she told me that she will do anything for a coffee. I told her I'd remember that if ever I upset her, or wanted to persuade her into anything...

I then left it for a day or two. We exchange a few casual texts then agree to meet for another coffee. This time I tell her I only have 30 minutes as I have another meeting. I sit her down and tell her to hold the table. Then I start generating social proof. I chat to everyone in the queue and a few people at surrounding tables with just general banter about it being cold, how a hot chocolate works around Christmas time, and good shopping before Christmas... usual crap.

I sit down and we chat some more, again a lot of kino from me. She asks me not to go to my meeting. I tell her that as much as I like her, she is unlikely to pay me for my time. She doesn't offer to oblige so I tell her I will have to leave.

I am then completely busy for a few days. We text but no meet ups. Late at night my phone rings.

HB: Hey baby, what are you doing?

Adam: I'm out. Family meet up, you know?

HB: I'm bored indoors and have had just enough alcohol to be really good company to you tonight.

Adam: Tempting, but unfortunately I'm out with family.

HB: What??!?!?

Adam: Yeah I mean it isn't the most riveting crowd, but sometimes you just have to do these things.

HB: Baby, if you wanted me you'd be here.

Adam: It's nothing to do with wanting you, it's about priorities.

HB: No one says no to me. If you don't see me tonight, then you can just forget it.

Adam: Fair enough. If you want me bad enough you will

wait until I'm back. Unfortunately I won't change my life for someone I've just met.

HB: As I said, if you want me you'd be here.

Adam: I didn't say I didn't want you, just that I won't be seeing you today. I will, however be free tomorrow night, I will see you then.

HB: Now or never!

Adam: Baby, be good I'll see you tomorrow night.

HB: ...(Silence)...

Adam: ...(Silence)...

HB: You know I'm just giving you shit right?

Adam: Yep. It's OK, I can handle it, but I think I may be too much trouble for you...

HB: Trouble how?

Adam: You'll see... I'll see you tomorrow night.

HB: Yeah, definitely see you then.

What amazes me is that we've had sex a few times since then and then last night we go through exactly the same conversation. She is constantly shit testing me to see how strong my frame is. She is great in bed though. I love slim, petite, black American chicks... I've had two girls from New York now and both had nipple piercings. Does this hold true for anyone else?

AFC AdamLondon

FR: Street game HB South African: November 07, 2006

Recently I have been doing a lot of approaches with the guys of the SOS [School of Seduction], in an attempt to refine my game.

Last Friday I was out with Trigger doing some street sets when I made a pretty decent discovery.

Trigger: Hey man wouldn't it be cool if we had mirrors so we could see the girls behind us as they are walking in the same direction as us?

AFC AdamLondon: Yeah, I suppose till then we can just look behind us... (I turn around and see HB blonde 8.5-9)

So I point to a flower brooch she has on her top, and say "I like that."

She is walking fast but smiles and says thank you. As far as I am concerned that means *please talk to me for a while.*

AFC AdamLondon; I mean it looks great, it says a lot about your personality.

HB: It matches my tattoo. *Shows me a flower on her arm*

We talk random stuff. I ask my AFC questions, like what do you do for a living, how work is going, etc.

Her phone rings. She picks it up, and gets into a lengthy conversation with someone for work.

Two minutes go by. I'm still walking with her. I look to Trigger who is filming the whole thing on his camera. He makes the "get the fuck out of there" sign, telling me I have been blown out.

I look to Trigger and mouth the words, "Nah, I'm about to close"

I am confident about this because as she took the phone call she reached out for my arm ever so gently, barely touching it. This told me she wanted me to stay.

Sure enough she finished the call and we keep talking. She apologises for keeping me waiting. I accept the apology, excusing her.

We random chit chat, then I close with the Party Close (I know it's a routine, but I love it). I then decide to text instantly. I don't know why, but I did.

It's amazing, It hooked immediately. It captured the whole moment of the sarge and continued through the next few texts. The texts are written below for reference.

Adam: Hiya HB, great chatting just now. People in London are usually too timid to talk to strangers. I didn't get the chance to ask, do you eat out often?

HB: I don't often no! What plans are you making in your head now? Or do I dare ask?

Adam: What kind of person do you take me for??? ;o) Actually it's probably better not to ask. Do you like eating out? I love restaurants, ever had Japanese?

HB: I love eating out and trying new things! Not really into Japanese but I love Thai! Why aren't you at work for the day? Or is chatting up random girls your job? [If only she knew, mwahahahaha]

Adam: How about you? Surely you aren't skipping out from your desk and sending texts... Shouldn't you be working? Working for myself has advantages :o) Coffee and lunches all the way. Thai, I haven't done that for a long time. Have you ever eaten in Busaba?

HB: Oy punk, I'm a hardworking city girl with only the best intentions at hand! Can't you quickly call? I'm getting bored of SMSing...

Adam: Hahaha, I love the attitude. OK OK, be good for a while and I'll call you when I'm out of my meeting. But only quickly, I'm a hardworking city boy :o)

I phone after two hours and confirm a day 2 at Busaba.

HB: Looking forward to Monday love - its gonna be interesting to say the least! Hope u have a great weekend and i'll see u soon.

I then ignore her all weekend and receive a text this afternoon.

HB: We still on for tonight?

Adam: I think I can squeeze you in ;o) As long as you behave yourself.

I then meet her and do the girlfriend thing. As far as I am concerned, nothing works as good as this for a day 2.

You simply pretend that she is your girlfriend. Hold her arm, help her cross the road, kiss her forehead when she says something funny, call her cutie and babe. This has never ever failed to get me my close.

Qualify, Qualify, Qualify! Can you cook? Do you clean? I'm looking for this in a girl (...), My last girlfriend did this (...), It's really not a quality I look for in a girl, what qualities do you have?

After dinner I ask if she likes ice cream. She says yes and I confirm that I will be paying for dinner and that she can pay for the ice cream. Off to Haagen Dazs... Mmmmm

Complete the date. She actually states halfway through, "I can't believe how close I feel to you, it's like we have known each other for ages." K-close, and DVD night at mine organised for Wednesday, where she is sleeping over on the spare bed.......

So I walk her to Green Park station and go home.

And as I am writing this she sends another text.

HB: Am home safe now luv. Thank you so much for a lovely evening and I'm looking forward to Wednesday! Sleep like the angel you are ... loads of hugs, kisses and of course, cuddles...

Hope this helps.

Meanwhile HB New York is sending me more shit tests via text.

HB New York: I am definitely gonna give you a hard time the next time I see you.

Adam: Hahahaha, some of us are still working. Be good, I'll call you when I am home. You have to wait.

By now I was getting recognized by people across the UK. A few people on other continents had noticed my results, namely a few top PUAs in Canada. After being particularly impressed with my game they wrote a very controversial post, which prompted a lot of people to question whether I was the real deal or just another scam artist.

AFC AdamLondon. The Man. The Legend BY SPIKE: November 09, 2006

I want to take the time now to recall my experience staying with AFC AdamLondon during mine and Crazy Serb's visit to London. Yes, that was months ago. Yes, that's how long I've been awwwstruck for.

This guy is fucking ridiculous. The first set I witness him open: he hooks, he dazzles, he solidly closes. I wonder to myself, "How long has THIS guy been in the game?" thinking he's one of those lifer's that dedicate their whole being to this art.

AFC AdamLondon: I've been doing this stuff ever since I bought *The Game* mate!

Spike: Oh cool, when was that?

AFC AdamLondon: 3 weeks ago.

You gotta be kidding me.

No he wasn't. And as I continued to witness him open and close successfully time after time, it was clear to me that he had something the majority of the Seduction Community lacks. Super Human Powers. I'm kidding of course, which makes him that much more amazing.

I keenly noticed that he was able to open literally every set imaginable, EVERY TIME. How did he do it? Did he say the exact right thing to each girl he came across perfectly every time? Heavens no. He would not be of this world. Instead, he says anything he wants and gets the same effect.

I had the unique experience of him asking ME:

AFC AdamLondon: Hey Spike, what do you think about opening up that girl with this?

Being flattered that he would ask for my opinion, I soaked in the moment of accomplishment, and proceeded to tell him:

Me: Yeah, yeah that might work (knowing full well that it was going work regardless of what he asked me for).

This is just the tip of the iceberg of what I witnessed during my stay with him. I was WITH AFC AdamLondon everyday to warrant this memoir of the occasion. You'll be hard pressed to hear him ever boasting or bragging. I've tried many times to tell him to his face straight up how good I think he is. But as I've learned, you'll only get the response of a TRUE champion:

AFC AdamLondon: I can't be that good mate, I'm an AFC

I was over the moon with the post. The aftermath went on for weeks, but from nowhere was this post refuted. There were just so many people who had actively witnessed me game and close that the sheer volume of replies nailed it. I was a PUA. Though I still felt like a little geek no closer to meeting my girl. Just a little more sexually gratified.

I was also trying to find loopholes, ways to speed up approaches.

Texting Cheat codes.. Moving the statistics in your favour! Revification method!: November 10, 2006

Ok Guys,

I have been experimenting with a whole bunch of stuff recently. Here's something I would love everyone to try.

I was sitting on the toilet staring at my phone wondering what I could do to improve my game... (Sorry for the graphic reference, it's the place where I get my best ideas)

Then I saw all the phone numbers of girls I have sarged over the last six months scrolling past on my phone and I remembered something one of my FB's mentioned after I broke up with her (she was falling in love).

She deletes the phone numbers of people she doesn't want to know. Now upon further inspection it turns out that many, many women do this.

So have you number closed a girl in the last six months only to have her stop responding to your texts? Odds are that she has deleted your number too!

This means advantage for Team PUA!!!!! We know who they are... they can't remember us, and after six months your game has probably improved a great deal. It's time to cash in on those old numbers!

I have been experimenting with different texts, and this is the set I feel has the best results so far.

This is a real text exchange between me and a girl that ignored my texts after number closing her in a club.

AFC AdamLondon: Watcha cutie, how's life treating you? Still partying hard or you getting too old for it now?

HB: Who is this?

AFC AdamLondon: Wow, forgotten already :o) I suppose thats how it is in media eh? I'm Adam, the PR manager. We met in Umbaba. You said to give you a call, but I've been busy until now. How are you? Still partying? ;o)

HB: Ah, hi hun. Yeah always, I'm coming into town tonight x

AFC AdamLondon: Cool, I'm heading to Chinas tonight with a bunch of the girls... where are you heading?

HB: Chinas too! See you there.

HB: Use this number in future hunni... (sends me a new number)

I've used a similar set on a number of girls now and its amazing how many actually start responding and really warming up.

So what to do with all those old phone numbers... don't throw them away. Why start with new girls when you can do a Blue Peter?

"Here's one I sarged earlier!"

Let me know how you all get on, then we can try and refine the texts to make them a little more solid.

I was also beginning to wonder how far I could push this. Would it be possible to close a celebrity? This thinking caused me to respond to a post on getting a celebrity with the following theory.

Re: How to Attract a Celebrity?: November 13, 2006

Upping your social proof is probably the only way you can be sure of getting a celebrity.

I have been working on my social proof game for a while now. Over the last few weeks I have been socially integrating myself with a group of FHM models I met. I am now invited out regularly by them and am often bumping into celebrities out at clubs.

You could theoretically use Social Proof + Game to hit on the celeb. You should try to find out which clubs and restaurants they go to. Cipriani in Davies Street has a high proportion of celebs. Build up social proof there and take it from there.

However, it is A LOT of effort and would take a considerable amount of money just to be in the right area...

If it's worth it to you, go for it. I'll be more than happy to help with anything including access to clubs.

AFC AdamLondon

I was beginning to really understand social proof and the value it offered. Having a large group of female friends to go out with is A LOT better than going out alone or with another guy. I was prompted to write this post on the importance of having female friends, who you DON'T try to sleep with.

Lets Just Be Friends on: November 18, 2006, 08:18:56 AM

Does anyone else find it odd that when the community go out clubbing we always end up in a large group of guys? To be fair, we will sometimes have one or two girls floating around whom we have sarged, f-closed, etc. But predominantly we are a large group of guys.

I think Style mentioned this in *The Game*.

For the last few weeks now I have been out with a group of girls I sarged. With one subtle difference I have not attempted to close any of them. I LJBF'd them.

I met this group of girls whilst out at Cafe de Paris and then Umbaba when it clicked that:

a) They would make excellent social proof, as they host club nights across London and always get the main VIP table and free drinks.

b) I would always have a good group of people to hang out with.

c) They are a bunch of attractive girls!

Don't get me wrong, it's great hanging out with the guys from the community, but how much so when there are only 2-3 of us and then 15 hot girls.

I've taken a few of the top guys out recently and we have had a really great time.

Why not try and LJBF a group of girls to go out with? I know many guys have spoken about it, but so few of them, as far as I can see, have ever done it.

Two of the girls in my group have tried to k-close me, which I managed to dodge. Now I'm the nice guy looking for "the one," which of course they all want to help me with. So every new girl that comes along for a night out gets introduced to me with a massive DHV from my girls.

Give it a go, try not to close the girls.

AFC AdamLondon

Something was happening. I was teaching a lot more and I realised that a lot of my stuff was becoming more and more complicated. Whereas I was more interested in the exact format of what causes attraction, many of my students were more concerned with how to get over a fear of approaching.

Technique for removing AA: November 18, 2006,

Hello! Boy, am I active this morning.

Okie dokie, someone once asked me why I have little hesitation when opening sets. For me the answer is simple so I thought I'd share a little of what goes on inside my head before an approach.

In my mind there are two types of approach.

1) The girls I don't feel attracted to.

2) The girls I do feel attracted to.

The first ones I am OK to approach, as should I succeed or fail,

I don't mind as I see little value in the set other than practice. I move up to them, touch them on their shoulder and start speaking. I have a number of set phrases stored in my mind to use in case I can't think of something situational. These are catch all's that would work on any set. Not necessarily well, but they will work most of the time nonetheless.

The second group are the ones that I expect give most people the problems. For me, I think to myself that if I don't approach here, I will be allowing my AA to grow. If I don't approach there is a 100% chance she will flake but even just approaching will reduce that amount, even if only by 0.01%.

So I force myself to touch them on their shoulder and start speaking. Here again I will either use something situational or one of my standard openers from the above situation.

The touching shoulder thing for me is key. Once I have touched them on their shoulder I have to speak.

I hope this helps somewhat. If anyone wants further clarification, just ask

AFC AdamLondon

Even as I was writing this post more people were becoming interested in the post on being just friends with some women. They wanted to know how I had built a social circle filled with a lot of girls. So I drafted a basic understanding of how to build a social circle.

Improving your Social Circle! A Step by Step Guide: November 18, 2006

Social Proof is one of the key areas in attraction.

If you are perceived as accepted by a social group then you have already gained a good deal of comfort from your target and can proceed to build rapport and close.

You can gain a good degree of social proof in a club or coffee shop, but this does not compare to a real introduction from someone who regards you as a friend. The good news? The majority of the skills you need to do this you will already possess having studied pick up.

Lots of people from the community have asked me how I managed to get success with women so quickly. It's really due to the fact that all the skills we learn to pick up I had already studied for about 8 years in my line of work as a PR manager... I just never thought to use them to get girls. (How stupid was I?)

So here's the simple tricks to reverse it. Sarge the social group as a whole;

SARGE THE PLANET!!!!!

1) Network, Network, Network. The more people you know the larger your group standing. Ask people what they do for a living. Ask for their business card or contact details as 'you never know when you might come in handy.' This is a really simple business close I have used on countless occasions, including with the Head of Intel UK, Head of Communications, Oscar Clark 3G phone network, Elizabeth Murdoch (Rupert's daughter), Martin Dodd, Head of A&R Sony, etc.. As you can see these are all real people who have massive value and yet were more than happy to hand over a business card, with their mobile number on, all for potential business and networking.

2) Organise a night out; invite all your friends, tell them to bring friends. Friends have friends who have friends etc. Organising a night out once every 3-4 months will really help you become more social and get used to leading the group dynamic. It is excellent for inner game, especially for the night you organise.

3) Join a club. A sports club, a movie club, a dinner club, a sex club, whatever you fancy. Meet people there and invite them to your nights out. Again, you are consistently building social proof and increasing the number of people in your group dynamic.

4) Don't try and f-close every girl you meet. Make friends, try and be picky; as your group increases you will probably find a whole bunch of girls are into you naturally. Hold off from the ones you don't want and wait for the girl you do like. If she turns up on a night you organised you will be in the perfect alpha position to do some serious damage.

5) Put people in contact with each other. This is a key part. Helping people has a big impact on social networks. Don't let others ponce off you, but putting people in contact with each other will help you stay the centre of all the interactions and continue to build your social proof.

A major key in my game is building social bridges. The more people I know, the smaller my world gets. I am now regularly bumping into people who know other people I know, and they all revolve around a few names. These are names of people I recognise but have yet to meet in person. However I know I will be meeting these people, and soon.

I am an AFC for life. This is a game, and I am merely a player.

But damn it sure is fun eh?

AFC AdamLondon

People were questioning how I had managed to get so good, and I was struggling to get across my exact method. I was relying on social proof as a catch all solution. That and inner confidence. Though they were powerful tools, I still didn't know why they worked.

Inner Game: November 22, 2006

I would say inner game is definitely the key to my ability to get girls.

Watching the pros you can see they all have strong inner game. It's a very integral part to what we do.

However, some people will build up that inner game through having routines to guide them through conversation. Others will do it via tapping. Some like myself and Jabba do it by assuming attraction.

As with everything, different methods will work for different people. Some swear by Mystery Method, others by RSD, and others like Juggler. The trick is to find a good method for each and every angle that suits you.

I will enforce what Magnus said about hanging with community guys all the time. It is very good in the beginning and even at social events. But too many cooks spoil the broth.

I always imagined the community to be a small bunch of guys hanging with a group of hot women. After I realised that this was not always the case, I began to carve my own niche. Read my post on upping your social network. But suffice to say, this evening I am out at Chinawhites with four of the best guys in the community, and 20 female pivots! This is my idea of a good night out.

If you guys haven't started doing it yet, then begin because I promise you this is one of the coolest things you can do. Girls begin opening and closing you. Mystery does it, Style does it. We should all be doing it. If you have a decent group of girls, strong inner game, and a good set of routines or natural conversation flow, you will have no problem getting girls.

AFC AdamLondon

At about this point the seduction school I was working for had gone bust and I had been approached by one of the original founders to work with him on another project. With my love for the game at an all time high I jumped at the chance. I also sat down to work out some common issues I had noticed amongst my students.

Leaving the School... November 22, 2006

Hi Guys,

I just wanted to stick a quick post up to let everyone know I'm leaving the School of Seduction. It's nothing personal, I love all of the guys at the school, and the last few months have been amazing. I have had the opportunity to work on pick up 24 hours a day, seven days a week. As humble as I like to be, if I were to say my game hadn't improved I would be lying.

I have learned a lot from the guys I met at the school. James Demarco, Tomcat, Beckster, Cryptic, and all of the others taught me a lot. However, due to a few personal reasons I have decided to step down.

I will still be working incredibly hard on improving my own game, and will be inviting everyone from the forum to work with me, so that we can all improve. I like the idea of improving my general lifestyle and social circles to improve my game and also wish to tighten my in-game flow to make closing more efficient. Not to mention cracking that threesome!

So guys I'm leaving the school but not the game. See you all in field!

Premature Eject-ulation. A common problem: November 22, 2006

Hey guys,

I've been doing quite a few private lessons over the last few weeks and have noticed a pattern amongst some of the students who have a reasonable amount of game but are still trying to find that hidden quality that appears to elude them.

The question to ask yourself is... Are you a victim of Premature Ejectulation?

What I am referring to is leaving a set prematurely because you "feel" you have been blown out.

I have witnessed a wide range of students now, some of them pretty well known amongst the community, who will quite happily open a set, get them hooked and run a decent number of routines generating a great deal of IOI's and then eject, actually saying goodbye.

A key point here is that this should not be confused with capture – recapture, whereby you leave the set on a high note at the beginning of the night, with a time bridge stating you will probably see them around later on and maybe they owe you a dance/drink whatever. This is so they don't feel trapped by you early on in the night.

I am talking about having a set hooked late into the evening and leaving the set for a number of reasons which may seem valid in your head at the time. However, upon further inspection, you can see that it would have made more sense to stay in set.

The common reasons I have heard are listed:

a) Run out of things to say

b) I was about to get blown out

c) It wasn't going anywhere

d) I don't know why I did it

Each of these reasons are an assumption based on the ideas of the PUA in question and not the girls in set.

a) Run out of things to say

If you have run out of things to say, go quiet for a while... but stay in set. I have field tested this and it is amazing how long you can just sit there not saying anything without getting blown out. Try it yourself. Catnap did a great game that illustrates this on my first ever meeting with the community where you ask a question and just freeze. The key point is that people are generally too polite to tell you to go away. As long as when you do eventually speak you say something worthwhile, you just look like you are enjoying the company.

b) I was about to get blown out

How do you know this if she will blow you out? Let her do it. One of my natural friends once asked me if I had ever been told the secret to attraction. I asked him what he meant and he said PERSISTENCE! Thinking back, a lot of the girls I have gone out with in the past before I got into game, I got by being persistent. Persistence can almost only ever exist with confidence. The more you persist the stronger your inner game can appear as long as you don't get too freaky... Stalker style.

c) It wasn't going anywhere

Again, see point b above. The only way you will know is to try it out. We almost always only learn from negative experiences. The more you fail the better you become.

d) I don't know why I did it

Again, it is highly likely to be a reason from above or something similar. The only exception I can think of would be a lack of attraction on your part, in which case fair enough. Why sarge a girl you don't like?

So think about it next time you are in set. A little bit of practice and living in that uncomfortable zone and you can put an end to Premature Ejectulation!

AFC AdamLondon

It was time to really push things out. I wanted the whole community in London to push themselves. With my birthday around the corner I set a challenge.

AFC AdamLondon's Birthday Party and Challenge! Cafe De Paris 2nd December: November 24, 2006

Hi Guys!

I am going to be holding my party on **Saturday the 2nd of September at Cafe De Paris in Central London** and am inviting **EVERYBODY** from the forum to attend.

There is, however, a nice little twist to help motivate you all and to hopefully make it a little bit more community driven. ***You may only attend if you bring at least one girl!***

To aid in this challenge I have arranged a deal with the club that **all girls who enter on my list before 11 p.m. will have free access to the club.** All forum members will pay a **subsidised entry of only £10** before 11 p.m., so hopefully it should be cheap enough for everyone to attend.

I would love it if as many people as possible could come along, and I will be writing a post up to help some of the newer members to the community with a simple routine set that should help them get their close.

A lot of you have been private messaging me with requests to come out with me, so please do make the effort to come along as it would be great to see you all there. Email me your names!

Best regards,

AFC AdamLondon

To aid in this challenge I created a first full routine set. It was one people could just copy word-for-word to guide themselves straight to an almost guaranteed close.

Party Close Routine Set! AFC AdamLondon: November 24, 2006

OK, here's a quick, simple set designed for people who have only just got into the community to get your first close. I thought I'd post it up to help as part of my B-day Party Challenge!

Opener:

[Tap them lightly on the shoulder. Don't give too much interest via body language, almost as if you are going to walk away and are talking to them as an after thought]

"Excuse me, I was wondering if you wouldn't mind giving me a quick opinion on something"

[Now I want you to use a justifier and a time constraint to hold them in place]

"It won't take a minute, and I could really do with an outsiders opinion. It's always harder to make a judgement when you are involved in the situation, wouldn't you agree?"

[This should start them on a yes ladder and get them opening up to you in a positive way]

"You see, my flat mates are kind of an item. I know, big mistake to start with, right? I wouldn't do it. Anyway.. recently they have been arguing constantly and, as far as I can tell, the main cause of the argument is which one of them is the bigger liar," (you have to love the classics... think of it as AFC AdamLondons revamped opener).

“He says girls lie more as they wear make up, use push-up bras etc... that’s all a form of lying. She says he lies more because he cheated on her... So, in your opinion, who lies more?”

[Try and get in as much kino as possible]

“Thanks for the advice, you’re really knowledgeable on things like this,” (if positive) or “thanks anyway for trying to help, its a difficult situation, eh?” (if dismissive) .

“It’s rare to meet someone in London who is so approachable, people here are often so closed. What do you do for a living?”

[This is a qualifier and a thread change... have a brief discussion with them, maybe apply a few routines, maybe try using conversation flow (i.e. Statement then Question) if you are comfortable with it. If you can’t think of any, don’t worry. Go straight to the close. I teach this set to a lot of beginners and you will be surprised how often it works without the filler in the middle]

Close:

“One more thing before I dive off... do you have a decent group of friends? [Don’t let her answer] It’s just that me and my friends go to a lot of big parties around town from time to time, only the decent clubs and we are always looking for cool people to come along.” [Qualifier]

“In fact, we are running a night at Cafe de Paris in a few weeks, have you ever been? Great club. We find that the bigger the crowd the better the party. Wouldn’t you agree?

“Plus on our guest list, girls always get in for free. You do have friends right?”[Negative and qualifier; this time let her answer]

“Ok cool, you should all come along, what’s the best way of getting in contact with you?”

I have used this hundreds of times and have taught it to almost all of my students. The success rate is really high when you get comfortable with it. In fact, so much so one of my students said it almost felt like cheating. If you haven't done any sarging yet it would be a great way to get started and then come along to a decent party and meet the community.

If you have any questions feel free to post them here. I'm sure a whole bunch of guys on the forum will have a few bits to add and refine it as well.

See how many hot girls you can bring.....

AFC AdamLondon

I'd begun to see patterns in failed sets of girls, and although I could almost always close, there were a few situations that made it almost impossible to get the number. Something referred to in the community as "Foolsmate Game."

Protecting Your Inner Game During a Day Sarge: November 28, 2006

Day sarging is very different to club game.

A key factor is the fact that during the day people have places to go; at night people are usually committed to staying at the venue for a decent period of time.

I am a firm believer in stacking the odds in my favour. Do a quick observation of the set before an approach.

Is she moving quickly? (Could be late)

Carrying heavy bags? (Unlikely to want to stop for a chat)

Talking on the phone? (Busy)

I know a number of guys who believe they should approach everything they see on the street. Now while this is probably true in clubs and bars, and potentially coffee shops, the street is different.

With a bit of calibration you can tell if someone has better things to do than randomly chat to strangers. Believe me, these women may not even stop for Brad Pitt carrying a cute puppy, asking them for their sincere opinion on an issue which only they could help him with, whilst performing a magic trick.

If you are building up your inner game then approaching these sets will just get you blown out and may damage your inner game, especially if you are one of those people who's inner game is built upon success.

Obviously it is better to develop a solid inner game to work from that isn't dependent on results. However, until then, stack the odds in your favour.

If your inner game is already solid, then why waste time on a set unlikely to hook? Unless of course you like the challenge!!! In which case good luck.

AFC AdamLondon

One of the most commonly used openers in the game is one where you stop to get a quick female opinion on something. Something I'd decided to make a conscious choice to stop doing...I'd come up with something else.

Can I Get a Female Opinion on Something? NO NO NO: November 28, 2006

Ok guys, quick post. Something occurred to me recently on a bootcamp.

How many of you are going around asking for a female opinion on something? This sets completely the wrong frame for the interaction! Think about it, why would you ask a complete stranger their view just because they are female? The obvious answer is that you don't have any girls to ask yourself!

Instead try asking for an "outside" opinion. Same theory but slightly stronger angle. Have fun!

At this point my game was getting more and more ridiculous. I wanted to really push myself.

FR Almost Threesome, Double Day 2: December 04, 2006

So I'm at the Church in Kentish Town two weeks ago and my voice is hurting after a particularly nasty session the night before at Cafe de Paris. So I figure... Hmm, what If I try opening without speaking?

Opener

[Tap on Shoulder, gesture wildly at my throat, stick my hand out]

[Mouth the words.] I have lost my voice, my name is Adam!!!

I open almost every female in the queue next to me waiting to go in.

My wing moves in and translates what I am saying. The whole scene is highly amusing as they try to understand my simple questions. Have you been here before? What's your name? Where are you from? Every time they get it wrong I'm negging them, every time they get it right I'm high fiving and hugging them. Kino escalation is growing rapidly with every set.

We enter the club and I open literally everything. The social proof is astounding, as I move around everyone is saying hi and saying, "Hey look there's Adam!"

I open a particularly cute set of US chicks and decide to go back to say hi after an hour or so. They hook.

I begin dancing with them. Two in particular catch my eye, a blonde and a brunette.

I start dancing with one, then the other, then both at once. I start escalation with first one and then the other. The brunette is giving me all the signs she wants to kiss. I hold off from the close...

... and dance with the other girl. Then she starts to move in as well. I still haven't even spoken.

I pull both girls into me and dance with both, then while holding them in my arms I k-close one girl holding the other in place. Then I turn to the other and k-close her as well. A few sexy dances later and then we triple kiss. They ask me to come back to their place after the club...

Damn! I'm thinking, this could be a threesome... then I remember, I have my LTR sleeping over my place. SHIT! She is coming down from Nottingham to see me. No chance of getting the F-Close.

So I stay in set with them, number close and confirm a day 2 with both of them the next day. What was really important to me was how I could keep up the threesome frame still k-closing the pair of them.

I managed to maintain the situation by gaming them as one. I used my standard day 2 routine of acting as if they are my girlfriend, but I gamed them as one. I was holding both their arms, kissing both their foreheads one after the other, etc.

Unfortunately, the brunette had to leave that evening so the threesome couldn't happen. However, the other one goes back to the US in January and I have been invited for a holiday.

Meanwhile I am seeing the blonde....but that is another story. I will be writing a post about it in the outer game section. This girl has a secret weapon.

Game!

AFC AdamLondon

Shortly after this the owner of the forum sent a message that he'd like to meet me for a coffee. Until then I had no idea how good any of the older members were and relished the chance to learn from someone more experienced.

I got some insights that would help shape a great deal of my future thoughts on the game.

Hard Vs Soft Skills: December 04, 2006

Hey Guys,

I was having a chat the other day with MegaMale and he made some incredibly accurate points which I wanted to share with the rest of you.

I stole this definition from a website...

"In the world of work, *hard skills* are technical or administrative procedures related to an organization's core business. Examples include machine operation, computer protocols, safety standards, financial procedures and sales administration. These skills are typically easy to observe, quantify and measure. They're also easy to train, because most of the time the skill sets are brand new to the learner and no unlearning is involved.

By contrast, *soft skills* (also called *people skills*) are typically hard to observe, quantify and measure. People skills are needed for everyday life as much as they're needed for work. They have to do with how people relate to each other: communicating, listening, engaging in dialogue, giving feedback, co-operating as a team member, solving problems, contributing in meetings and resolving conflict. Leaders at all levels rely heavily on people skills too: setting an example, team building, facilitating meetings, encouraging innovation, solving problems, making decisions, planning, delegating, observing, instructing, coaching, encouraging and motivating.

People skills are "hard-wired" in the neuronal pathways of the cerebral cortex. This means that at some point a behavior was repeated often enough that neurons grew dendrites that reached out to other neurons to make the connections needed to make behavior pattern automatic."

Complicated, eh?

Actually, not really. The key is understanding that soft skills are generated by guidance and practice, with reinforcement. Old views and behaviours can't simply be deleted. Instead you opt to follow the new patterns as you learn them. Introducing a new skill is difficult as the old ones still exist, and from time to time you will access one or the other randomly, though this will happen less and less as you reinforce the usage of the new ones.

Without this practice or reinforcement, the new skills become dormant and it is easy to lapse back into the old ways.

"This is why a program of lectures, group exercises and handouts —even a week-long course personally conducted by a world-famous celebrity author— cannot by itself provide enough reinforcement to establish the new pathways needed to change ingrained behavior patterns. Without reinforcement, even people who want to change are likely to return to their comfortable patterns, and so dysfunctional behaviors remain the same."

This is why a community such as this forum is incredibly important. The different methods have their place, but neither is necessarily better than any other. The key is finding the one that works for you. Some people may find they are more than comfortable finding the basic information they need online and then going on a bootcamp or workshop to concentrate on practicing and reinforcing the new behavioural patterns.

This is why many people feel a low a few weeks or months after a bootcamp. Without the reinforcement of constant practical applications, the neuronal pathways disintegrate allowing the soft skill to revert to a state similar to the one it was in before the creation of the new pathways.

So guys remember to keep practicing! We're in this together. All of us.

Wow... How heavy was that for a Monday evening?

AFC AdamLondon

I discovered that you could pretty much get anyone to do anything if it isn't made into a big deal. The second you put weight into performing an action it suddenly gains a level of value and makes them think twice about performing it. The Ice Cube routine really helped illustrate that for me.

Ice Cube K-Close Routine! I used it to get a threeway kiss! December 07, 2006

Ok guys, I was out last night with a pair of HB's and their friend. I used this routine to get a threeway kiss and thought I'd share it with you.

Dare the girl to hold an ice cube in her mouth... Then tell her to give it to you.

You need a good bit of comfort first, but you'll always need that. I then pulled another girl in and passed the cube to her.

Give it a try and let me know if this works for you guys too.

AFC AdamLondon

Finally the challenge was on us. My birthday had arrived. I was amazed with the amount of people that turned up, and the amount of girls – somewhere near 30. It was the best birthday ever and finally the geek had found a home.

Re: AFC AdamLondon's Birthday party and Challenge! Cafe De Paris 2nd December: December 11, 2006

Hi guys I just wanted to say a big thank you to everyone who attended! You guys are all the best.

Since joining this community I have never felt so accepted or welcomed in my life. I have made some of the greatest friends including all of those who attended on the night, whom I haven't met before.

If anyone else has any more pics please feel free to post them, so I can save them on my computer.

All the best,

AFC AdamLondon

Then a put up a random post on philosophy. The funny thing is, this has stuck in my mind ever since and I constantly quote it to students.

Re: Who is your hero?: December 14, 2006

My hero has to be Spiderman.

I know it's weird but I love the way he deals with all of life's problems with a quick-witted remark and just gets on with it.

Plus, you all know I love the whole *with great power comes great responsibility* thing.

I told a philosophy student I was gaming that one of my favourite philosophers was Peter Parker, and then gave the quote.

She's like wow, thats really cool... I've never heard of him.

Then I told her about the whole Spiderman thing and she was really impressed.

AFC AdamLondon

I mentioned in the almost threesome that I'd met a girl who had game. Well she sure did and at the beginning of 2007 I spent more time with her than any other girl. I was growing tired of the random girls and appreciating those with a bit of game a lot more than a random hot bimbo.

No place to bring the girl.....: January 03, 2007

HAPPY NEW YEAR!!!!!!

Ok this is my first post of the New Year, so I had to add that first. I hope you all had a great break and are looking forward to improving game in the new year with all those New Years resolutions.

I had been receiving a lot of phone calls just before Christmas asking about escalation and common problems. However, after a lot of analysis it turns out the key issue was that many people just didn't have somewhere to bring the girl. Unfortunately this was something I hadn't had a lot of experience with, as I have had my own place since I was 18.

Soooo... I thought I'd experiment.

Introduce HB Finance Manager of Citibank.

She is a cute blonde chick I pulled at some club last early December. She is in her mid 20's and earns a good sum of money. My mission: close her without using or mentioning my flat (so I theoretically could have lived at home with parents).

The game was pretty standard so I'm not gonna post it here. In summary, I opened with social proof, ignored her for a while, came back and qualified, stuck around in the set, closed with the restaurant close and then day 2ed.

The restaurant is where it got interesting. I made it clear to her that I believed in fairness through dates. Many people have that awkward moment of "...should she pay ...should I pay?" Instead I told her I prefer that I pay for the dinner and she can cover dessert.

Quick equation:

Adams favorite day 2 restaurant: Tokyo Diner. Meal for 2 = £14 - 16 approximately

Adams choice of dessert: Haagen Dazs Ice Cream Fondue = £18.95 (I like ice cream)

So after the ice cream, (lots of kino throughout) we head off to HMV to browse movies. I point out a few good ones, as does she. Finally I show her a movie I really like (*Plunkett and Mclean* if you're interested) and we agree to watch it sometime. I take her to the station and she goes home.

Next we exchange a few texts and I agree to meet her at work for lunch. We do a simple lunch and in fairness I can see the risk of this becoming too friendly. Friendly and me ending up with an LJBF. I realize I have to get to her place, and soon. I tell her that we should definitely do the movie thing soon, which she agrees.

I then very calmly but firmly tell her that we should do it at her place. She responds with, "Oh yeah?"

I continue. "Yeah... the thing is I'm too used to my area, I think its cool to go somewhere else... Like an adventure. And besides, it'll be easier for you to get to work." She lives within 2 minutes of Centre Point. The night is confirmed and I leave with a quick hug.

On the night of the date I call her to let her know I have everything ready and to see if she would like me to pick up some dinner. She tells me she has already eaten and is looking forward to the film. I then tell her that it is actually getting pretty late and that it looks like I will have to sleep over.

HB Finance: What?!?!

AFC AdamLondon: Yeah it'll be like a slumber party. It's just that by the time the movie finishes it'll be too late to get the train. (I told her I was working late so it's already 9:30) And I don't do buses. Besides, I'm a well behaved man who is fully in control of his loins... I'm more worried about you jumping me... you do have a couch right?"

HB Finance: Yeah...

AFC AdamLondon: Well then its all good, I promise I'll be well behaved, and besides it means we don't have to rush the movie. [WTF does this mean? Movies have a set run time... But it appeared to work]

HB Finance: I'm still not sure...

AFC AdamLondon: Look I need to know now, as I've got to bring all my stuff. I'll make it easy for you. I'll bring everything and come now... I'm hoping you aren't so cold that you'll leave me outside your doorstep freezing all night.

HB Finance: Haha, OK OK, I'll see you soon.

AFC AdamLondon: Cool.

Off I trot to visit her. I make a quick call on the way.

"It's OK we're safe. I've left the condoms at home so you won't be tempted to jump me

HB Finance: Hahaha, you think you're funny.

I get to her flat and we start to watch the movie. First half and she is as cold as butter.

AFC AdamLondon: So I bring the movie over... I bring you chocolate chip cookies... I think you owe me a hug. Your flat is cold.

I pull her in and get the hug. By the end of the movie she is sitting in my lap like a kitten and I've been stroking her hair all the way through.

We go to bed. I run my usual closing game.

And now the moral of the story! Three days later I am leaving her place for the 2nd time, at 7:30 am.... I walk past GAME in Canary Wharf and they have bloody Wii's in stock!

I queue for like three hours and then manage to grab one for myself!! I ended up spending all Christmas playing with my LTR and the Wii!

So guys, remember: girls don't always mean relationships and sex... Sometimes they lead to the latest video games console!!!!!

Have fun guys. As usual, any questions feel free to ask!

AFC AdamLondon

I was queried as to whether this was cutting it a bit fine and risking getting LJBFed myself.

However, by now I was so congruent with playing by my own rules, it was never an issue. I did need to find a way to break this down though.

The following post was in response to a question one of the guys on the forum asked about me getting LJBFed.

Re: No place to bring the girl..... January 04, 2007

Hey Taylan,

Yeah there was a risk of getting LJBF'd as I wasn't running my normal game. I had slightly miscalibrated. I am usually very cocky funny, and often kino escalate a lot.

Example: Stare behind the girl as we first start to walk on a day 2...

HB: What are you looking at?

AFC AdamLondon: I'm just checking to see how cute your arse looks.

HB: OMG, are you serious?

AFC AdamLondon: It's OK... it looks cute. (pat bum)

HB: Did you just touch my arse?

AFC AdamLondon: Yeah, but it's OK... don't look so shocked, it's a nice arse. Anyway, we're nearly there now.

I almost always change threads quickly after pushing the bar.

My normal close is telling them I never have sex with a girl on the first night as this is a strict rule which I never break. This is so important.

So many girls have slept with me first time around and said "Ahhaha, so it looks like you CAN be beaten! I always get my man." Aww shucks, she got me

It always starts with sitting up chatting to them and looking into their eyes. Then I go for the triple kiss routine to get the k-close if I don't have it already. Then kino escalate, stroke their neck, etc. If they pull away or give any negativity, which I have to admit is rare (I find if you do it right they are so horny they rarely pull away), I try to pull back a bit or tell them to slow down if they start to get into it. This preempts them pulling away.

But if they do pull back I just go back one stage to kissing and then building it up again.

If they ask if I'm trying to sleep with them or say, "what do you think you're doing?" I respond with:

"Nothing!" or "I'm just kissing you... your lips look soo good right now," and then kiss them again.

Then I just build it up naturally through touch.

Hope this helps. If you want more info regarding this just private message me.

Oh, and in regards to drinking, unfortunately I don't drink. Still most of my game once I have them indoors is all kino based anyway. I find no matter what you say to them, as long as you're touching, speech doesn't matter. Stroke their neck, kiss it, bite it, stroke their back, pin their arms above their head... hold them close and kiss them. From there, it's on.

Also, I have had a lot of success by asking them what their views on multiple orgasms are? In my honest opinion, this line is GOLDEN!!!!

Have fun

I hope this helps,

AFC AdamLondon

I was now being quizzed for all types of variants of my game from the standard practices others use. I was being acknowledged, in London at least, as doing something slightly different. I still didn't really see it and was getting a bit daunted by it all. Yet still my love of learning and teaching pushed me forward to crack just what it is that makes us attracted. I knew what to do, just not why.

Triple K-Close routine: January 09, 2007

So we all know how awkward it can be to go for the k-close. Even those with a lot of experience sometimes misjudge and push for a kiss without enough comfort. Next thing you know you have created an odd vibe between you both and its time to kick that frame control into overdrive to save the situation.

I have a tendency to get overly cocky funny. When I first started out I found it quite uncomfortable to use standard k-closes that involved speech as I would often make the situation a little too funny rather than seductive. Because of that I came up with this little routine, which I have used ever since. I also know of a few top PUA's who also use this routine.

Ok, let's say you have built the situation up to a point where you think it would be OK to go for a k-close. Maybe you are sure, maybe you aren't. Either way, you can give it a go.

Wait for a moment when she says something funny or emotional. Create it if need be. What you are looking for is a point in the conversation when emotions run high. At this point say something like;

"Wow, thats amazing!" or "Aww, come here you!"

Then give her warm hug with both arms wrapped around her and then, kiss her on the cheek. (Kiss number one)

Lean back, but keep you hands wrapped around her slightly, maybe holding the sides of her arms. Lean in again, this time to kiss her other cheek. (Kiss number two)

Maybe emphasise this by placing your hand on the opposite cheek from the one you wish to kiss, or by her head. Make sure you are going to kiss her cheek and not her lips, unless its blatantly obvious she wants you. You should be watching for her body language. Did she angle her head towards you? Did she close her eyes in passion? If so, then you can be pretty sure she is ready for a full kiss.

If she gave some indication that she definitely did not want to go for the full kiss, perhaps angling her head away from you, or moving back slightly, then you can simply take a step back and continue building comfort. Then try the same routine again later.

If you did get some positive signs or couldn't assess properly then go in for another kiss back on the first cheek you kissed.

(Kiss three)

This time, however, make sure you go via the front of her face. This enables her, or you for that matter, to move in for the full k-close if it "feels right."

Again, if it doesn't feel right you can simply move back and begin building comfort until you are ready to try it again.

This way you should be able to judge how much comfort you have generated without giving the game away.

I once went in for this only for the girl to give no signs of interest. I backed out and suggested meeting up during the week to see my favourite restaurant and get her phone number to make it a date. After the number close I repeated the routine and this time all the signs were there.

Sometimes you can be so close to having the correct amount of comfort but be just shy enough to get the close. This way you can judge it a little easier.

I hope this helps guys! If you have any questions ask away as usual!

AFC AdamLondon

One of the most amazing things about the game is the incredibly funny situations you end up in. I think there is something about exposing yourself to so many different people (excuse the pun) that makes you more likely to run into those incredibly funny situations. This was one where I just wish someone was filming.

Lip service, Brothels and HBJapanese: January 11, 2007

Hey guys,

I don't tend to post these that often but I just had to share my day

2 with you all. There is not much to learn, but what a day! As many of you know I have a weakness for cute little oriental girls. Last year just before Christmas I see this very cute girl walking in the opposite direction to me and got her by going direct. I've summarised my direct close as I don't think I've posted it before. Personally it's given me the best success rate out of the different direct methods I've tried.

I initially walked past without saying a thing to her, then commented to James DeMarco, who was with me at the time, that she was incredibly attractive and if I had more time I would have gone for it. We were both on our way to teach at a bootcamp. James then said, "Who cares if we are late? If you want her, get her."

Who could resist when it's put that way?

So back I trot. (This could be seen as neediness, but if you frame it right in your head, going back to a girl can be used in your favour.)

I approach her with a quick tap on the shoulder than speak.

"Hey, I really only have a few moments, but I saw you walking past and thought you looked interesting."

I go to walk away..

"Anyway, listen, I really have to go to this meeting. I would like to text you though, what's the best way to get in contact with you?"

She couldn't get her number out quick enough. Cute chick, nice figure, beauty technician with a strong Japanese accent. Perfect!

And so that was it. I invited her to a club one day with about 20 other HB's, spent 20 minutes chatting to her, and then went off with another girl, some blonde if I remember rightly. Spent most of Christmas and New Year with my LTR and HBNewYork.

Then figured I could do with a change of scenery, so I text

HBJapanese.

“Hey cutie, wanna go clubbing tonight?”

She says yes. I organise her guest list entry but don’t bother to turn up. Next day I text her to see how her night was. She responds

“Very good, but I didn’t see you!”

I respond “Nah I was too busy with work, however we can lunch on Thursday if you would like.”

And so the stage was set.

Everything was pretty much to book. I tuck her under my arm, we fluff talk, I kino, I stare at her arse. She pulls me up on it, I tell her not to be ashamed of a cute arse. She tells me off again, I do it again, etc.

Then we head to St James Park to see the scenery and to get caught in the rain apparently. Any girl that will romantically walk with you in the rain at a slow pace taking in the scenery as if it isn’t raining wants you. - Extract from the school of the bloody obvious IOI’s.

Then it starts!

We are walking past Buckingham Palace, by the guards in daylight, in the rain.

HB Japanese: I think you are handsome

AFC AdamLondon: I think you are cute

HB Japanese: Lip service?

AFC AdamLondon: *CHOKE* I’m sorry what?!?!

HB Japanese: You know, lip service... you understand?

AFC AdamLondon: Erm... I think so

HB Japanese: You don’t understand.

AFC AdamLondon: I think I do

HB Japanese: Come with me...

She proceeds to walk towards the park.... Naturally I follow.

HB Japanese then pulls out her English-Japanese translator. Punches some buttons into the screen and pulls out an answer

FLATTERY!!!

AFC AdamLondon: Yeah yeah that's what I thought you meant Hug and triple K routine.

Man LMFAO!!!! I literally wanted to piss myself with laughter. It was so hard to keep a straight face, but bugger trying to explain that situation to her.

Then literally 3 minutes later we walk past a children's playground and she stops to point at the toilets.

HB Japanese: Brothel?

AFC AdamLondon: *muffled laughter* Tee hee hee.. I'm sorry what?

HB Japanese: Brothel?

AFC AdamLondon: No, its a toilet.

HB Japanese: Brothel.

AFC AdamLondon: Well sometimes I'm sure it is... but honestly its primary use is a toilet.

HB Japanese: Sorry?

AFC AdamLondon: It's a toilet.

HB Japanese: No not toilet.. Brothel... on tree!

AFC AdamLondon: OHHHH BLOSSOM!!!!

HBJapanese: Yes, romantic.

AFC AdamLondon: Yes, yes it is...

Man, it was all so funny. I just had to share!

AFC AdamLondon

I had become obsessed. I knew I needed to do something about it but wasn't sure what.

Reflection: January 11, 2007

Look at me, I was sarging 24/7. In a way I still am... but not in the same way.

I had party girls all over me, was having sex with four different girls a day and then had a change of ideas. Things got into perspective. Who was I proving myself to?

In my head I was still trying to prove to all the kids that picked on me at school that I could get a girl, many girls. I finally realised that I had reached a point where I was happy and that it had almost been the end of me.

Now I've taken a step back. I game, but not over anything else. I analyze them, but don't feel I have to close. I spend more time with my LTR and my friends and am genuinely happier. When I go out I go out with party girls and a few mates, build up social proof and have a good night out, but am only doing it two times a week at most.

The rest of the time? I'm either working, playing on my Wii or playing Dungeons and Dragons! I've started a campaign again.

Good friends, work, hot girls and geeky games. I'm a happy man, for now at least.

What I meant by a change in my sarging habits was the fact that I was now organising nightclub events. I had been approached by a number of nightclubs in London and a large promotion company known as LondonParties. They had noticed that when I went to a club I was always surrounded by beautiful girls. They asked me if I wouldn't mind bringing them to the clubs on a regular basis in return for a small fee and free entry. Wow, I was actually getting paid to social proof.

Still, there were many guys who couldn't even get into the clubs to meet the girls in the first place.

Re: West End Guestlists: January 13, 2007

I organise a lot of guest lists. Actually, many people don't understand the trick to getting into a club, so below is a list of the general rules.

1) Don't wear casual clothes. No trainers or jeans.

Now this can be translated as you can wear jeans as long as they are dark and trendy, but definitely no trainers unless you are an organiser.

2) You must bring at least one girl for every guy

The reasoning behind this is to ensure that there is a decent supply of women for everyone to reduce fighting. It's kinda a big rule, hence the problem you are having getting into clubs. Personally, I hate clubs with too few women. Use a party routine like the one I gave for my B-day last year, it's easy to get girls in that way.

3) If your name isn't on the list, you aren't coming in.

In London, being on the list doesn't mean free entry. It means you can come in. Literally if you aren't on a list in advance you can almost forget entry. I organise many guest lists, unfortunately I got inundated with requests from people that I couldn't manage it. I am currently working on a system with a good friend, when its in place I'll let you all know.

4) Don't be late

At the start of the night, most clubs worry that people won't turn up, although they always do. It's a constant fear, so they tend to be more lenient on entry at the start of the night. They tend to open at like 10 p.m., so turn up early. It's easier to befriend the bouncers that way too, as they aren't up to their eyeballs in peeps.

5) Don't assault the staff.

These guys have a tough job, if you get aggressive with them, or backchat them whilst they are working, you will ensure that you not only don't get in, but that you may never get in even if on a list. If you are friendly to the door bitches, they will eventually warm to you, then access is easy. Make their night easier and they will help you.

Hope this helps guys!

Have fun,

PM me if any questions.

AFC AdamLondon

There were now a good number of really decent posters adding value to the forum, and in response to a particular one on dealing with flakes, I put in print my standard follow up to reduce flakes. At the time I remember swearing by this text.

Re: Flakes: January 17, 2007

Flakes are a pain in the arse.

I find the easiest way to get them to show is to never truly let on about the meet. Let them feel like they suggest it. My standard first text is.

"Hey cutie, so random meeting you just now. Are you always so friendly to strangers?"

Then I add some random question at the end. Usually I ask

if they go out often, which fits into my life frame. I find it's important to lead them throughout the texts, never commit to anything, and show them how much of a busy life you lead. If you are not responding straight away its good to give a reason. Most girls are aware of the "don't reply right away thing" so giving a reason. It allows you to drag out the responses and makes them believe you are genuinely busy, especially if you are arranging a meet up. The words *maybe* and *might* are your best friends.

"Watcha cutie! You won't believe what has happened to me over the last 24 hours. Lets just say it involved 3 work meetings, 5 glasses of vodka, 2 late night cab rides and a penguin. Anywho, I'm going out a couple of times to celebrate this week, but might get a few hours spare at some point. How's your week looking?"

Notice how I didn't directly invite her out... Normally she will suggest a time she can meet with me, or something like;

"I'm busy this week, I can't make it. Maybe next week?" at which point you can take it from there.

However what if she responds like this...

"Nah, sorry I'm busy this week"

You can reply with.

"Haha ha, you wish! I wasn't offering. If I get a few hours free I'm going to use it to chill out. I love how you were pretending to be busy though. In fact, me and my mates were saying just this week people don't tend to lead interesting lives outside of work... so what do you do that's interesting?"

Reframe and Qualify. I keep this reframing up right through to the f-close.

Hope this helps. If there are any questions, PM me.

AFC AdamLondon

Though realistically the real reason many people were failing in set was their personal hang ups. There were issues which we all had. I had some really big ones which I wanted to come to terms with. I realized I never let them interfere with my game, but I did really want to sort them out.

Something big became apparent to me. I was attracted to Americans. It's silly, I know. But there was something about the way they were so outgoing and made a real effort to be...well, hot. The girl from New York who I spent a great deal of time with and a group of other US party girls that I went out with regularly were gradually swaying me to begin looking across the Atlantic. First I had to face my own demons. Living with them wasn't enough for me. I'd have to actually remove them.

Why should she be comfortable with you, if you aren't comfortable with yourself? January 23, 2007

Here's something I used to teach on the bootcamps we ran last year. I figured I'd share it with you all.

Everybody has aspects of themselves they "feel" let them down. We all have things about ourselves we would like to change.

Here is a list of my perceived issues.

1) I have a double chin.

2) I have crooked teeth.

3) I have an odd body shape.

4) I have a blood disease that effects my immune system and skin, causing it to break out in boils.

5) I have a visible spare rib (ironic with my name being Adam and all).

There are probably more but I can't think of them right now. The fact is I have accepted them as they are part of me.

Some of these things I can and am doing something about. I get braces in 3 weeks! Some of them I can't or are too costly to fix. The fact is that when I am in set, I don't think about these. I have dealt with my personal demons and I'm OK about them.

When in set, sometimes it's easy to think about a personal issue. Does "such and such" look bad, or am I "such and such" too much? These subtle signals are given across to the target and can seriously affect your results. How can you act confident whilst hiding your mouth? Realise that you aren't the only one with issues. Everyone one of us has problems from the hot girl with the bad accent, to the cool guy that has dandruff.

This is the main reason why negs work. They remind the target that they are human as well. Most people aren't rude enough to actually point out a fault. I have heard many people detailing what to say when someone points out a fault.

HB: You are short.

Guy: What is it you like about short people?

Why does that answer work? It works because it shows he is comfortable with his faults. He doesn't see them as faults, they are his strengths!

For example, a few weeks ago I was out with a friend. He explained that for years he felt that his height was holding him back with girls. He was 6 and a half feet tall. This guy is huge and skinny to boot! Within moments I told him that his height is an advantage in so many settings, from reaching the top shelf to watching for oncoming predators!

Sure enough I see him in set no less than four hours later. He is gaming a hot blond who has lost her friends.

Friend: You look lost.

HB: I can't find my friends.

Friend: No problem, describe them to me. I'll find them with my super powers.

He then proceeds to tuck her under his arm and wander around with her as she describes her friends to him. He reunites them and leaves. Sure enough 20 minutes later she is dancing with him and sucking his tongue out of his mouth.

The key is that he had become comfortable with that which he saw a weakness.

There is an old phrase from fencing.

The good players identify their weaknesses and hide them, showing no weakness and crushing their enemies!

However..... The phrase doesn't end there!

The BEST players identify their weaknesses and use them, turning weakness to strength and disguising strength amongst weakness.

I feel this works well in game.

I live in Mayfair, but I never drop my personal address to a girl when I'm gaming her. At least not in the first few instances. Once I have done all the hard work, I use my address as a subtle drop in the conversation, letting them learn where I live and then they almost invite themselves back to my place. Rather than me rubbing it in their faces and risk putting her off, I let them grab hold of one of my "trump" cards and let it work without forcing the issue.

I don't show my teeth when I smile in photos; it's a subtle thing, most people never notice.

I don't want a reminder of how bad I look. When I'm with a girl I laugh out loud showing my teeth, because when it's just me and her alone, I am comfortable being who I am. It's all I know how to be.

Be comfortable being you. Hope this helps!

AFC AdamLondon

Still my concept of Social Proof was growing in my mind, and my execution of it was surpassing even my own beliefs.

Insta-Social Proof. Twice the Speed half the effort!: January 25, 2007

Hey Guys,

I was out at a party earlier this week, bit of a fancy do. One of my PR contacts invited me, so I thought I'd bring a few friends and have a play. However, here's the rub. For someone who has built up their own social proof over the last six months in their environment, how was I to get that same effect in a new place.

For those that don't know, I have made myself a bit of a someone on the night club circuit in Central London. I'm not important or anything, I just know enough people so that were I to walk into a club alone, I would be bound to spot 2 or 3 groups of hot girl friends, or important guys that I could hang with. These people stand out from the rest of the crowd because they have private tables if they are guys or are wearing little clothing if they are girls.

I often get opened by girls in these clubs just because they want to know who I am and ask how I know everyone.

Now, what is there to do in a situation where you have no previous grounding?

The main route to do this would be to speed around the club saying hi to everyone, doing short sets and then building it up. However I knew the night was due to end within 2 hours.... and there were a lot of people, some who were incredibly into themselves. How was I to cut some of the erroneous effort away and get to the nitty gritty? Well I tried something that night, kinda on the fly and it paid off, big time. To be fair, I've only tested it once, however I feel the premise is strong and that it would work for others. As always, I will only know if you guys give me a hand testing it, so here goes!

I enter the club and quickly ascertain which group has the highest perceived social value. I spot them sitting in a corner alone surrounded by the loudest women and a few important looking people. I take my wing Jim Stark, and our friend into the area and we chat to each other.

Now we are surrounded by a few small groups of people chatting, say around 4 other groups of 3-4 people talking. Big groups always break down into smaller groups of people when in conversation. There is a formula for this if anyone is interested let me know. Anyway, the idea is that from a distance, other groups would see us as part of the group.

A few small openers later just to make us appear part of the larger group and BINGO! I get opened by a hot blonde.

HB: So what's your name?

From here I used standard escalation and the usual techniques. I made sure to introduce her to my friends so that it looked like I was bringing her into our group. She did ask who the others were and I simply responded with "Ahh, they are the rest of our section." She didn't probe further; if she had I would have just qualified her.

She hangs around for a bit. Then we bring a few more in, open a few of the main group and the next thing you know we are all closing left, right and centre.

The key point is that although I didn't "have" the social proof, it appeared like I had it, and that was almost as good. It's just important to ensure that you don't look like you are outside of the group, rather that you are a part of it. Small gestures like getting one of the group to put your drink on their table or asking for a lighter can help to show this.

Anyway guys, give it a try! As usual, if there are any questions, just PM away!

AFC AdamLondon

Meanwhile my game had surpassed that of my poor flat mate who was there during the stripper incident right at the beginning, though he was trying to improve himself. He came out with us a number of times and created some classic lines, which really captured the essence of what it was like to be out with him.

I've often thought that the real reason I got good was not that I pushed myself, but because my wing man was good looking and a natural at blowing me out. So with that massive handicap I had no option but to find sound ways to attract girls. Otherwise he'd get them.

Wise words from AMOG Scott: January 26, 2007

AMOG Scott is my flat mate, and to be fair to him he has learnt a lot about not AMOGing and game over the last few months.

From time to time he comes out with classic lines that I seriously love, and I thought I'd share with you.

HB: Why did you just say hi to us?

AMOG Scott: Why are you being rude? I came here to be friendly and say hello, and you are just being rude. That's appalling behaviour.

HB: Can I meet you Wednesday night?

AMOG Scott: I'm playing video games with my friends but you can come and watch if you like?

HB: I love eating ice cream

AMOG Scott: It's all fun and games until someone gets fat!

His frame is incredible. Game with this guy and it is guaranteed to help you improve. Sink or Swim.

AFC AdamLondon

Then a drastic change came over me. I had a phone conversation with an old friend of mine that made me realize something. The lines, the games and tricks...they aren't as important as what is going on beneath the interaction. Girls WANT to sleep with us. The trick is proving you're the right person for them.

Be honest, do you lie? January 26, 2007

There is a power to be had in telling the truth; especially to someone you want to build a deep relationship with. In a LTR people are more likely to be accepting of behaviour others may deem unacceptable. Especially if framed the correct way.

I received a phone call from an old MLTR the other day. I haven't spoken to her for a while as she now lives in LA. She is one of the girls who know everything about me and my other girls. During our conversation a small incident took place, which I thought I'd share.

Personally this girl is an easy 9 to me. And I love that US accent. Oh, I've brought this up before as well, she has a nipple piercing, as do half of the US chicks I've met... is this like a US thing?

Anywho here's the interaction:

HB: You know the fact that you do all this seduction thing just makes me think that every time you say something nice you are just schmoosing me.

AFC AdamLondon: I don't say nice things to you to schmoose you. I'm not hiding the fact that I'm going to ravage your body the next time I meet you, or the fact that until then I will be fucking other girls. I tell you nice things when you deserve them, or they fit, because I like you.

HB: You see Adam that's what I like about you, you don't chat shit. You say it as it is. We have to hook up again soon.

Literally after she said those words I realised there is an unbelievable power in just being true to yourself. Girls appreciate the honesty. I use this all the time in business and PR. If you don't know something or a particular situation is going bad. Don't hide it. Just be honest, everyone appreciates it more.

Especially girls who have hundreds of guys lying about the fact they sleep around.

In fact, I met a girl a few days ago; in my mind she wasn't particularly attractive but she was a cool girl so I stayed in touch as mates. She starts telling me about a guy she is seeing. She shows me a text where the guy is fumbling around stating he doesn't know how he feels for her, he needs time to address his feelings they shouldn't see each other too often, should have separate lives but still do dinner, etc.

I said to the girl, if he came straight out and said, we've only just met, let's take this slow and still see other people what would you say? Her answer.

"I'd be cool with it. I don't know how I feel about him yet, but hell we're young."

So I reconfirm; so basically if he just came out and said it you'd enter an open relationship with him?

She replies. Yep.

But he didn't and doesn't have the guts to say it, and won't get what he was angling for. Now I'm not saying this is true for all girls. But definitely for some. In my experience it's the easiest way to get MLTR's.

AFC AdamLondon

It was amazing. You could tell the truth and still build up the required attraction! There was something that was required. Some formula, or way of behaving that made them want you, irrespective of whether you were seeing someone else. You didn't have to lie, you could be completely open with them.

Rather than using routines, or lines, or even chasing the girls – I was noticing that I was actually becoming attractive.

Getting Negged! January 26, 2007

Hey Guys,

Last night I had an amazing night with a cute chick. I'm going to write a post up about it later as I pulled her into a social proof trap.

However, the funniest thing happened. She negged me. Like not an insult or shit test but a real neg. She obviously felt she needed to do it to build attraction. I've noticed girls use a lot of our techniques naturally as they try to game someone they feel has higher value.

As it's good to see things in a positive light I thought we could all share them together and laugh at them. Remember I told you all my issues with my funny body shape? Well... Here's the neg.

HB: You know you have a pretty good figure, for a FAT guy!

Anyway, What is the funniest neg that has been used on you?

AFC AdamLondon

By now my understanding of the power of social proof was ridiculous. I was seeking ways to use it in other aspects other than just opening.

Social Proof Trap - HB Jockey at a Model party: January 28, 2007

I am starting to seriously love social proof game now.

The more I analyse it the more congruent it becomes with who I am. I am currently finding it an asset to my life that doesn't take away from other activities, nor does it require me to learn extensive routines or refine my skill. I am far from perfect, however, there are many, many more levels to reach. I am looking forward to reaching these. However, as each step not only increases my ability to get hotter and hotter girls, it also helps me with my professional life.

So with that in mind I wanted to show you guys a sarge that I personally feel is a marker in my progression through game.

HB Harriet: she is a semi-professional jockey, an excellent dancer and has a pierced belly button, but no nipple piercings... ahh you can't win them all. What she lacks in make up and bleached hair, she more than makes up for in sexy innuendoes and intelligent conversation.

The Setting:

www.nnmodels.co.uk

I sarged the owner of this company in Umbaba. I opened her friends in the queue with Ninja and James1. I used capture/re-capture on them inside and got introduced to her in the club. I LJBF'd her for access to the models rather than a straight close. We had a few lunches and I taught her how to do her own PR. She took me out for a lovely lunch on my B-day and, between you and me, she has become a really great friend.

Now she invited me to the official launch of her model agency...

The Target:

I am sitting in Chinawhites alone. I was tired of dancing with the princesses on the tables and just want to chill. HB Comes up to me and says, "Hey you, anyone sitting here?" We fluff for a while, she comments that she has seen me dancing with everyone and wonders who I am. I'm getting used to this now, I can afford to be completely unreactive and chilled. From time to time girls walk past, and bouncers/promoters say hi.

She comments, "Wow, you really do know everyone." We dance, she asks for my number as I'm not a weirdo like the other guys hitting on her in the club (her own DHV). We exchange and that's it. I was with her for less than 10 minutes.

After a few conversations with Harriet I can tell that she fancies herself as pretty high value. She drops hints about winning tournaments, teaching prize winning horses, only dating rugby players, etc, etc. She negs a lot too and says I must be soft as I'm a city boy.

It's all erroneous, the fact is she is about to be placed completely out of her league.

The Trap:

I invite Harriet out to a small do a friend of mine is throwing. I tell her to dress nice as its a launch of my friend's company. I get her to arrive one hour after we get there. She turns up 30 minutes late...

I arrived at the party with a journalist for my friend, a magician I know from the club circuit, Jim Stark and TomCat. We sarge the room. What do we open with? Well most people we are introduced to by an excited Natalie.

The others...

"How do you know Natalie?"

Most HB's reply that she is the owner of the model agency I

work for. When they ask us, we respond best friend. Voila! Instant rapport and comfort. So we move around the room. This really isn't effort at all. We are either showing magic tricks, talking business or eating free food and drinks. It's fun to meet all the different people and learn about what they do, including the professional belly dancer who was up on stage.

When she finished I got introduced to her by my friend. The dancer turns out to be a legal secretary by day. I tell her she has to meet my friend Jim... who closes.

Then Harriet arrives

When she arrives, she spots me in the club. I am currently chatting to two of the models from my friend's agency. She patiently waits as I finish my conversation. I raise one finger to let her know I won't be long.

We go to the bar to have one quick drink. She is incredibly nervous. I calm her, fluff talk, then tell her I have to go mingle for a little while longer as I'm still "working" but I'll be back. I introduce her to my wings to keep company while I go off. I move around the room, chatting to the few more people I want to chat to collecting a few more phone numbers from some girls. Then finally go back to H.

She says ,"I don't want to get in the way of your work"

"No problem" I say. "It's my fault for leaving you, I didn't mean to be rude, just had things to close. Anyway, there isn't anyone in here right now that I would rather spend time with other than you, as long as you have something interesting to say," and I nudge her.

We talk, we dance, she drags me to a couch, we hug, she kisses me, she is all over me, we stand she pushes me to a corner and grinds up against my lap.

I tell her it's time to go, she mentions it would be easier to stay at mine than travel all the way back home. I tell her that despite that being so, I don't believe in sleeping with someone I'm not completely comfortable with yet... I tell her she'll have to work harder to build comfort. She drives me home, and then takes herself home. I get phone calls from her all night and the next day and every day since.

It isn't that she was amazingly hot and it wasn't that I ran amazing game. What happened was I had given myself so much social proof, I didn't need to game. I didn't need to believe I was the prize. I *was* the prize. I could buy her flowers and she would have loved them, I could buy her drinks and she would still have been all over me. I could have been silent and she would have carried the conversation. I could have taken her home and fucked her and she would have done it.

No effort beyond being sociable and myself, mingling with people in a room, having fun and eating and drinking.

Hope this helps guys.

AFC AdamLondon

How to win friends by being genuine: January 29, 2007

Hey guys,

LondonHunk just sent me a quick PM asking me to share something, which I appear to have neglected in my recent posts on social proof.

Friendly Closes.

How do you go about closing someone as a friend? I think the key part here is to understand why you would close them as a friend. It may appear to some on here that all I do is go around influential people chatting to them running game and getting numbers of people to get free access to clubs.

The simple truth is, that were I to do that I would get nowhere. Imagine how many cute chicks run straight up to a manager of a club and ask for his mobile number to hook up with him and then ask for free drinks, access to a club or a free table.

It's all about being social. I genuinely am a friendly person. I like people and I like helping people. Last Saturday night I ended up at a guys house with a groups of HB's. He invited them to the house and they said not without Adam (FR coming up). Anyway, it turns out the owner of the house is related to Matthew Freud, the guy I used to work for in PR. But I didn't learn this until after I got his number. Getting someone's number after you learn who they are can look suspicious.

So how do we get the number?

Easy peasy! Chat for a while. If it's a guy you should have loads to talk about such as girls, games, football, etc. Then say, "Hey man, we are always going out clubbing... I'm big on networking.... Can you send me those photos of the night?... Let me help you with (previously mentioned problem) when I'm back at my desk..." Then number close.

At this point keep chatting and after a while they will gladly divulge who they are.

The key here is that you didn't chat to them to get something from them, you chatted to them to be friendly and then got a number to either continue being friendly or to help them.

So how does this work in relation to clubs?

Allow me to explain how I got my contact at Cafe de Paris. I noticed that guys ignored this one girl who wasn't particularly attractive, so I started chatting to her. She introduced me to the email girl, who was bored. When not in set I would chat to her.

After two months of random chat I told her about game. She was intrigued and told me about her man problems. I taught her how to qualify and "be the prize." She started telling her friends about me and they invited me out to a club.

They were my princesses. Hanging around them I got introduced to the event organiser of the club. I helped him with a few PR contacts I had and now we are friends. I didn't chat to the first girl to get "in" with the club. I didn't know any better. I was just open and outgoing.

I now regularly help out with club events, as a kind of hobby.

I didn't plan it. I could probably engineer it, but it wouldn't have had the same impact. I wouldn't be as trusted as I am. Forget making the connections, just make friends.

The best way to do that?

Be friendly. The rest happens naturally.

AFC AdamLondon

....

I had recently gained a wing. At the time he was known as Jim Stark but now he is known as MrM. He would become one of the biggest driving forces in my game. Working with him we began sarging again in earnest. In fact, we began sarging four days a week, every week for four hours a day. We were trying to push each other to be better and better.

Our ideas were bounced off each other and with another person analysing as much as me we broke things down even easier.

Re-Framing: February 01, 2007

Hey Guys,

Me and my wing Jim had a good chat yesterday about frame where he sat and defined frame as *the underlying assumption that defines an interaction*. Now Jim has some incredible game. In my mind it is some of the best I have ever seen. We got discussing the idea behind reframing the situation.

Now our earlier thoughts were that you can take their assumption and then apply a template, i.e, "I am the prize," and filter their reality through that template.

For example.

HB: I'm hot, I have a boyfriend, I'm the prize and you can't have me...

PUA: OK, how does that affect me? Why should I care?

So you can see that the assumption of the PUA is that *he* is the prize and he ignores the girls idea that she is the prize, no matter how much "proof" she brings to the table in terms of being in a relationship, having a girlfriend with her, etc.

Now, I'm sure this works a lot of the time. In fact, I have used it myself. However, we have altered this slightly to encompass a much larger crowd.

Bare with me. *ahem*

So the assumption of the girl is *this guy is hitting on me* or *I am the prize*. This is her frame. This may or may not be said, but it is underlying throughout the interaction. She maintains this as long as she can, and is congruent with it as it is her life and her view.

What if our assumption were different? What if instead of just assuming we could get her, we added a deeper level? What if the PUA not only assumed he could get her but that he had an assumption that her frame was a small part of his?

I've tried to create a simple process breakdown for this which I've added below.

Identify

Spot her assumption, whatever it is, and then break it down. If she assumes you fancy her, try and ascertain why. Is it based on her looks? Does she have a strong personality? Is she the leader of her group?

example 1: *This guy fancies me, but he isn't getting me*

example 2: *I have a boyfriend. I will flirt, but then go home to my man*

Empathise

Make references to the fact you have spotted it, but subtly. This is kind of like a cold read. Make subtle hints towards the fact that you have spotted her assumption. You will start to shake their foundation as their assumptions are about to be proven wrong. This will break down the world around them and leave them open to a new suggestion of what the underlying assumption is, one you will create.

example 1: *"You know, its weird how girls automatically assume that a guy fancies them just for talking to them"*

example 2: *"It's funny how you can tell someone is in a relationship just from looking at the way they hold themselves"*

Absorb

You should then seek to show them a glimpse at your frame to begin merging their little frame or world view into your own. In the first instance below you can see the girl's frame being absorbed into the PUA's frame as he absorbs her assumptions into his and shows her his assumption or frame is that all girls assume he wants them and that they should be so lucky.

example 1: *"Its terrible really how girls assume that a guy fancies them all just for chatting, I suppose some guys can't get girls and get really desperate chasing after every little thing they see."*

In the second example the PUA is beginning to beat on her for being in a relationship. He is absorbing her views and her relationship into his frame. He is becoming a voice of experience, and when she buys into his frame he will be able to assert a level of control over those views.

example 2: "Its the way a girl holds herself. I think a lot of guys may have trouble seeing it, but I know to me and my friends it's easy. I suppose maybe it comes with experience of women.

Reframe

I will give the examples of reframes in a second, but first we have a simple template reframe. I'm not saying it doesn't work, rather that the reason behind it working is deeper and if you understand it you can tailor it to more varied situations.

HB: "You fancy me, but I'm not going to have you"

PUA: "I can see you fancy me, what is it about me you like?"

Here is a full reframe. This is the most important part of the reframing process and does require confidence as now you shape the new context of the interaction and she buys completely into your frame. In the first example the PUA has completely removed the issue of her assumption that he fancies her, and has restructured the conversation so that now she *should* see him not only as the prize but will try to qualify herself into this frame by inserting more effort into the conversation. This enables him to be seen as the prize by others and, more importantly, by her.

example 1: *"Sometimes I just like to meet someone who is actually interesting, capable of holding a decent conversation and knows how to have fun without them trying to get hold of me all the time"*

*example 2: "For example, lets look at that girl (*someone you can see has a boyfriend). *See the way she is subservient to her man? How she looks to him for validation before speaking? It's the way most women are with men in relationships. It's due to the fact that the man knows he has her and starts to assert his control over her. Women respond to this on a really deep level. Obviously there are exceptions, but these are usually when a man is comfortable enough with himself that he doesn't need to control another being to make himself feel good."*

You could realistically take it any way you choose, after all it's **YOUR FRAME.**

I hope this helps give some insight into what me and Jim are working on at the moment. By the way guys, be careful with this stuff. It can be really powerful if done correctly. Remember in everything, you should always be sure to try not to hurt other people. We aren't in this to be arseholes.

I gave an example of a girl with a boyfriend however, personally, I don't touch girls with boyfriends unless they have made it clear it's an open relationship or it's about to end, before I begin doing anything with frames.

As my favourite philosopher, Dr Parker, said, "With great power comes great responsibility."

There is a whole heap of other stuff. We have only just begun to clarify it all, but all of it has been field tested. It's just about finding the best way to write it down so that it is easy to explain.

Hope this helps,

As always, any questions feel free to ask

AFC AdamLondon

Re: Wise words from AMOG Scott: February 13, 2007

AFC AdamLondon: Man, you know a drink in Cafe de Paris can cost around £1,000 for a decent bottle.

AMOG Scott: Man that's crazy. In my country you can get ten high class hookers for that price!

Man these are the moments life is all about.

AFC AdamLondon

Improving Myself

Something had to happen. I realised if I was to get the American girl of my dreams something would have to happen. I was finally going to have to face up to those inner demons and vanquish them. If I wanted the girl of my dreams, I'd have to be ready for her.

AFC AdamLondon - Facing up to my inner demons: February 13, 2007

Hey guys,

I just wanted to add a quick post here for myself more than anything. I don't know if any of you remember the post where I talked about my personal issues with my appearance.

Well, today I took one step in the right direction. I now have braces. For the next two years I will have difficulty speaking due to a slightly unorthodox position of the braces and will over salivate when chatting to HB's. LOL.

It's something I have always wanted to do and thanks to this forum I have done it.

I got an amazing deal on a special set of braces that can't be seen by the casual observer. So guys, here's the start of the transformation. Only two years to go.

These are my goals:

1) Get straight, white teeth

2) Make money; *at least* £60k a year

3) Buy a piece of property

4) Start and maintain a regular fitness programme

5) Gain regular host nights at clubs across London

I'll add to this post if I think of any more, however I think these are the key ones.

It's nothing to do with game, for me its all about being able to smile in family portraits and show my teeth. Besides, they're all paid for and hooked up now. I have a bright set of train tracks in my mouth!

Through game I made a decision to improve all aspects of my life; from relationships to appearance to work, everything.

I don't just want to understand how to generate attraction. I want to *be* attractive. To have an attractive lifestyle. Not for HB's, but for myself.

This is it. It's the first step and commitment to being the person I want to be. In the past I have spoken a lot about what I will do and this is the first step to actually doing it.

This is why I love you guys and why I have the confidence to do what I want. There will be no failing along the wayside. I shall not falter. I am not worried about being lonely or rejected. I can take a step forward in the direction I choose knowing I have good friends and support behind me.

AFC AdamLondon

No matter how much I changed my personal self, I still posted and shared my tips.

Re: Games: February 16, 2007

I use a little game where you can analyse the persons personality type based on the way they hug.

Me: I'm really into psychology.

HB: No way, really?

Me: Yep yep, I love all those psychological tests. You know, the ones that really show you everything about somebody even when you have just met them.

HB: Wow, do they work?

Me: Yeah, it's amazing how well.

HB: Show me!

Me: Nah.. you're too nosy! Besides, it would weird you out.

HB: It won't weird me out! Show me, show me!

Me: Ok, well basically you can tell a lot about somebody by the way they hug you. Especially if you don't know each other very well, that way they can't fake it. So go on give me a hug.

Hb: Ok

Now she will invariably hug you with both arms, at which point you can fluff about her being quite confident in social settings, especially when she has mates with her.

Then point out that normally a stranger would only hug you with one arm around your shoulders standing side by side, so she obviously feels comfortable talking to you at least, etc.

Hope this helps,

AFC AdamLondon

But still it's important to remember; no matter how good you get... there is ALWAYS someone to put you in your place.

The Nature of the Beast: March 01, 2007

So last night I'm out at China's. I'd just finished a day 2 early and thought I'd hook up with this girl I knew would be there.

I got to the club, k-closed the girl and she had to catch the last train home, but I thought I'd stay in the club. I head over to my usual table, only to find out my girls have been moved. So I move over to them and they quickly invite me to party with them.

I jump up on the table and start grinding with a couple of the really hot ones. I build up a bit of kino.....then WHAM!

A massive bouncer pulls me off the table and two of them strong arm me away from the girls.

Bouncer 1: Sorry mate you aren't allowed on that table.

AFC AdamLondon: Hey buddy. Nah, it's cool, I work with the club.

Bouncer 2: Yeah we know.

AFC AdamLondon: Ok... I bring pretty heavy guest lists here dude. What's the deal? And why aren't the girls on our table?

Bouncer 1: The owner of the club invited the girls to sit at his table. He doesn't like you dancing with them.

Bouncer 2: Enjoy your night.

AFC AdamLondon: No problem guys.

I then walk straight onto another table and chat to some other girls.

...However, talk about AMOG.

I would love ideas on what to do about that. I didn't even see the owner. The promo guys apologised, but obviously their hands are tied. If I had seen the owner I would have gone and chatted to him, but to be fair I don't even know what he looks like.

I always believe in being humble. Specifically because of situations like this. There is always someone bigger and better out there.

On the up side, I know he didn't close any of them. He should sign up for a bootcamp.

AFC AdamLondon

At this time, I had a massive discovery. I had created a project with my best wings. We consolidating a company that specialised in bringing girls to parties. It was expanding on the guestlists I was doing before.

I also noticed that a lot of wannabe PUA's were pretending to have game, but only getting results when they were teaching. I looked into it and found a pattern.

Have you noticed??? March 12, 2007

I've noticed this before and am aware that a few others have noticed this as well, however I thought I'd post it for the benefit of those new to the community, or those who may still be wondering...

Why can people get incredible results when running bootcamps or events?

It's because they are the leaders of the interaction. They have the highest level of social proof, are the alpha male and are leading. You name it, they are portraying it.

This is of course a generalisation and there will always be exceptions to the rule. However when you think it through it's easy to see why people who try being an approach coach can then get incredible results in comparison to a normal sarge.

Now is this an attack on peoples' game? Am I insulting newbies who are trying to pass themselves off as PUA's?

Not at all. In fact, I am pointing out the fact that there is something here for us to learn. There is a reason why the leader of a social interaction is often seen as the most attractive, and there are ways of spotting the leader (and of course engineering a situation so that you look like him). However, the key fact is that you should be leading your own interactions!

Those of you who have been to more than one bootcamp and are still frustrated with the results, why not try organising a sarge yourself? You could limit the people on the sarge to, I don't know, say six guys. You could then pass on the basic theory to the newbies whilst getting in some valuable practice. Not only would this increase everyone's access to the knowledge, especially to those that maybe can't afford a major bootcamp, but it would encourage more meet ups, whilst finally giving you, the organiser, a massive dollop of social proof to play with.

If you want an example of situations where this works, look at the recent field reports in The Church. Spoons game definitely improved a lot quicker once he started organising the sarges with his wing.

I personally noticed a massive change in my game once I started working as an instructor.

Look over the posts. Look for the patterns. See how people's game dramatically increases if they are organising a sarge or bootcamp.

I suspect this is why a lot of people feel comfortable enough to organise their own bootcamps and new businesses as soon as they get pretty decent at game. Once they try running their first bootcamp they will be able to perform incredible demonstrations to their students. Now the better bootcamps will have the experience and knowledge to help you calibrate and get the results you are looking for, whereas the not so experienced ones may struggle to explain why they are so good. They will have just vague ideas and suggestions designed as "catch all's" to try to help you. This is something to watch for, no?

It isn't all to do with social proof either. I suspect an equal portion would be down to your mindset. You being responsible for organisation would give you the correct frame to enter the interaction. You would probably adopt a more alpha outlook in general as people look to you for what time to meet, and fears over whether they will get into the club.

Don't take my word for it, look through them yourself. Then get out there and organise a sarge. What have you got to lose?

As always, any questions feel free to ask.

AFC AdamLondon

I was also beginning to notice a pattern forming in my openers. The ones that were working from cold approaches in the street seemed to have a pattern of working from comfort initially. Though I wasn't sure how much.

Re: Best Openers: March 14, 2007

Picking up strangers isn't a "natural" way for us to meet a partner. There are a lot of studies at the moment looking into what causes us to become attracted to others, and one of the key elements is the comfort that is gained through meeting someone through a common group.

When approaching a stranger you need to combat that with something that will cause them to overlook this fact.

1) Generate a lot of comfort instantly, which you then break to cause attraction.

2) Be alpha so they are submissive to you.

3) Be interesting enough that they hold around to learn the rest.

I'm sure there are other ways to get strangers, but right now it's the first thing in the morning and my brain isn't in gear yet.

In short, an opener used on a complete stranger in the street needs to either be delivered very well or be interesting in itself.

You are finding a good result with the soft opener first as it gives a reason to talk to you. Also, the advice they give you is a deposit. This deposit makes them feel (somewhat) tied to you, enabling you to get your foot in the door to do a standard opener.

I hope this helps. If you want to know more, PM me and I'll start a new thread.

AFC AdamLondon

An interesting question with regards to getting a kiss started to remind me of one of my best kisses. It reminded me of the importance of remembering to be sexual. Without any form of sexual escalation, the interaction is doomed before it starts.

Re: Kiss close issue: March 16, 2007

Here's my advice to properly escalate a kiss.

Invite her to your house for dinner and a movie. Do it via text if need be. Make sure you escalate it correctly, though. When you're at your place, turn the lights down low, hold her through the movie and absentmindedly stroking her hair or neck. That should be more than enough kino escalation to get a k-lose, and it should feel pretty natural.

AFC AdamLondon

Re: Kiss close issue: March 16, 2007

OMG, I just remembered my best kiss ever!!!!! We were watching *Beverly Hills Cop 3.* I was 15 years old. Our heads were moving so slowly towards each other in anticipation of whether we were to kiss. It was so awesome, neither of us were sure as to whether we would kiss. It took like two whole gun fight scenes before we made out.

She left me a month later for the following reason:

"I really like you Adam, it's just that we've been together and you just aren't moving quick enough for me. I need to have sex ,you know? Anyway I've started dating Steve. You know him? The young guy at the butchers."

It was still a great kiss though

AFC AdamLondon

Though by now, my game was evolving into something else. I was actually becoming attractive. It was beyond what I said to the girls. More and more I found they wanted me.

I'll get by with a little help from my friends + Mystery's K-Close routine: March 18, 2007

This post is not what it seems at first.

So I was out last Saturday night with 3 students, Tom and another instructor. We hit Cafe de Paris and mixed it up between hanging in the VIP area with the Princesses and the main room. Every time we hit the table I would take the time to explain to the students what they could try to improve on their last set and flirt with a pair of new princesses. I had got both of their phone numbers before, but had never bothered chasing or doing anything. I had plenty of social proof as the new girls had only just started hanging around the Princesses of which I am now seen as a regular.

I pretty much ran a simple Dance-Kino-Escalate jealousy routine thing on them. Anyway, at 2 a.m. we finished teaching for the night. One of the two girls went home, so I sat at the table with one of the students and the other girls. The night pretty much went as standard. I barely spoke to the girls, occasionally danced or posed with them for a photo. Though I spent more time talking to my friend Lizzie and the instructor who is a really good magician.

Anyway, when the night finished we all made for the door. At this point I turned to the girl and said:

AFC AdamLondon: Do you like American pancakes?

HB: Yes

AFC AdamLondon: I think I'm going to go home, do you want to have some with me, Leon (instructor) and my flat mate?

HB: Ok cool, sounds like fun.

So Leon, HB and I all head to mine to meet my flat mate. Then the plan unfolds. At my street Leon decides he is going to meet a girl he knows in the area and leaves us alone (cheers mate!). And we hit my flat.

We wake up my flat mate, play music, cook pancakes and eat them. Then on cue my flat mate says, "I'm tired I'm going to bed. I'll put the music on in your room if the two of you want to keep listening to it." (Cheers mate!)

So me and HB go to my room. I show her some books, we chat, then I say I'm gonna nap for a while as I'm tired. She lies on my arm and we turn out the lights. I'm not even bothering to escalate. The simple fact is we both knew that something was on the cards, and I was tired. I could always get her in the morning. **Then it happened....**

HB: Do you want to kiss me?

AFC AdamLondon: I'm sorry what did you just say?

HB: I said, do you want to kiss me?

AFC AdamLondon: I know that one.

HB: I'm sorry what?

AFC AdamLondon: I know that line, Mystery made it. There's no real way out, he he.

HB: What?!?

AFC AdamLondon: I've thought about it, but decided I didn't want to muddy the waters with our friendship and the other girls. I'm not looking for a relationship.

HB: Neither am I? We're young enough to just enjoy ourselves without any commitment right?

AFC AdamLondon: .....

I then move in for the kiss.

What fun eh? Sometimes the girls close you... man, I feel sorry for the girls we game. I actually felt played by this girl...abused almost. She basically pounced on top of me after the kiss and practically forced me to f-close. I feel dirty. Though in a good way mwahahaha.

AFC AdamLondon

This attraction was growing and it was becoming easier and easier to get the girls I wanted. I no longer needed to mess around with lines and was experimenting heavily with Direct Game.

Go Direct - what do you have to lose? March 21, 2007

Hey guys,

Once again I've been out practising some sarging techniques in an effort to improve my game as much as I can. This week I have been mostly looking at Direct Game.

Personally, I feel there is a lot to be gained from going direct if it is done in the correct way. Not only do you cut down the time it takes to sarge, but you remove a lot of the chance of getting LJBF'd and, in my experience, if they do give you the number they are much more likely to go all the way.

In the last week alone a lot of my closes have been done direct. I think this is due to the fact that I'm not scared of the rejection you will undoubtedly face, and also because I am becoming increasingly bored with having the same conversations with strangers. Not that I don't love the game, just that I'd love some more of these girls to actually have something interesting to say about themselves.

Personally I have developed a set routine, which I think works the best. I am fully open to other's ideas if they can improve on this, as it is something I am still working on. But at present here's the game.

1) *Force an IOI* - Maintain eye contact with every girl you are interested in. If they meet your eye, smile. If and when they return the smile continue to walk a few steps allowing the moment to pass and then...

2) *Approach* - Walk back towards your target. It doesn't matter if you approach from behind in my experience or appear to be chasing after them. You are trying to build one of those "movie moments."

3) *Confidence* - Do not appear to waver in your resolution to talk to this person. Don't speak too fast, be confident and don't stumble the words out of your mouth. If you have scared them by approaching from behind be sure to laugh over it and apologise for scaring them. They will often join you in the laughter and this actually increases your chance of success.

4) *The Line* - "I'm sorry to bother you, it's just that I only have a few minutes as I'm on my way to a meeting, and I knew I'd kick myself if I didn't speak to you. You look really interesting, what's the best way to get in contact with you?

5) R*esult* - Sometimes they will say they have a boyfriend, sometimes they give you their number. Either way, be friendly and courteous. If they give you email, pull out your phone

and start typing it in... This is a pain. After a few seconds of attempting say, "You know what, my phone is a pain with this. Give me your number and I'll text you.

And that's it. Fast, simple and painless. I was discussing with my wing the other day; if you have sufficient social/entourage game built up, the chances of this succeeding is even higher, as you are approaching from a position of perceived higher value.

Give it a try, what have you got to lose?

Even ten sets would take less time than one good, indirect set.

Let me know how you get on.

AFC AdamLondon

Re: Wise words from AMOG Scott: March 27, 2007

Hey guys,

I am still laughing from this comment. I gave my flat mate Scott two free tickets to the P-Diddy event this evening. Having no idea of the cost of them he gave one of them to a random girl he met 3 weeks ago.

Today I realised how much they were worth and told Scott, just so we could laugh about it. Then his girl called....

HB: Hey baby, I just found out how much those tickets cost...

AMOG Scott: I didn't know how much they cost, though I just found out.

HB: You must really like me.

AMOG Scott: No I don't really like you that much. If I'd have known how much they were I wouldn't have invited you. I'd have sold them.

LMAO
HAHAHAHAHAHAHAHAHAHAHAHAHAHAHAHA

HAHAHAHAHAHAHA

AFC AdamLondon

The sets continued, one after the other. With more and more girls coming into and out of my life, whether they had guys with them or not, it didn't matter. I was unstoppable, but still something ached at me. Why was I doing this? The more I did the better I got.

Selective hearing/reading/whatever: March 28, 2007

Hey Guys,

I thought I'd post this email trade I've been having with a girl I met last week at a club. We were flirting with each other across the room, we spoke briefly, but then I closed some girl I was with. She closed some guy. Then we got talking and her poor guy came up to me to confront me because he wanted to get AMOGed. He told me that since I was trying to steal his girl I should buy him and his girl a drink. I informed him that she looked too young to be drinking, and that I would never steal his girl because it isn't fair to take a girl off of her boyfriend. As for all I know he may not know how to get another one. Then poured him and his girl an orange juice and let them go.

The girl then came up to me later to confirm that he was not her boyfriend and would like to have my Myspace address. I got bored recently and decided to push for a Day 2 with her.

While writing I realised that there are essentially two conversations going on. It's as if we are oblivious to the fact there are two separate threads. One is about random day-to-day rubbish and the other is the build up to the Day 2.

My mum always said I had selective hearing. I think with regards to game it is highly beneficial.

Adam: So what plans do you have for this week then, shorty? Anything interesting going on?

HBHannah: Well, I'm really not sure... relaxing. I might pop down to Paper this evening for the P-Diddy party, but I'm not sure. To be honest, last week was very hectic so I'm just sticking to bars and restaurants during this week. And it's still too early to be planning for the weekend.

What about you, anything interesting going on? x x

The next day...

Adam: Hey cutie. I think I saw you yesterday in the P. Diddy line. Did you go in?

Bars and restaurants sound fab to me. Do you eat Japanese food? I'm at Chinawhites tonight, Aura on Thursday (possibly) and definitely Paper on Friday.

HBHannah: No I didn't go. Me and a friend ended up in this random bar for the evening. I was just way too tired to go out. I lurrrrrrrrv sushi! I may see you on Friday then, I am meeting a couple of girlies there with my mate before we go to another club... xxx

Adam: You probably did the best thing last night, it wasn't worth going. Have you ever eaten at Tokyo Diner? It's one of the best Japanese restaurants I have ever been to. Yeah it'd be good to see you this Friday. Are you bringing your boyfriend?

HBHannah: He is not my BOYFRIEND! He is a friend of a friend....... No, I haven't been there, whereabouts is it? I may go if it really is that good.... xxxxxx

Adam: Hahaha, You are easy to wind up... Tokyo Diner on the other hand is the 2nd best restaurant in London, with Maggie Jones taking the top spot. I go there all the time. Do you ever get evenings free? Perhaps next week sometime I'll take you. If it won't upset your boyfriend that is... he he heJust thought I'd share. As usual, if there are any questions just PM me.

AFC AdamLondon

Funny story about tonight I thought I'd share: March 30, 2007

So somehow, probably through poor planning on my part, every single girl I have successfully closed in the last 2 months is coming clubbing with me tonight. Along with my LTR.

This includes:

A princess (the party girls) I took to bed after promising myself I wouldn't sleep with any of them

An American girl who has only slept with one person before, and likes me because I don't drink

An American girl who is in the same group of friends as the one above... and the one above doesn't know

A girl I have been sarging on and off for the last 4 years which finally came to a close

A 27-year-old girl who used to date a guy that bullied me at school and who wants to get back with her

A girl who I met randomly last week at Paper and is coming out specifically to catch up with me before moving onto another club

It doesn't include:

The police officer from last night.

It also includes:

A girl that flirted with me to piss her bf off

A girl that swears we have slept together even though we haven't

A girl that grabs my ass whenever we dance yet nothing has happened yet

Angelina Jolie

OK, I lied about the last entry, but the rest are true.

I'm normally very careful about ensuring these things don't happen.

I think I have allowed it to happen out of curiosity, to see what will happen. In fairness, I'm probably just gonna be social to all of them and just enjoy a good night of flirting. None of them really strike me as the type to be overly possessive, unless I give them a massive reason to be.

If I get all of them in bed at once I will officially be quitting the community, and selling the video on e-bay for $3.99

No point to this post really, just wanted to share.

If I don't write anything in the next four weeks, it's because I have been attacked simultaneously by all of them and am nursing a bunch of broken limbs and a mutated penis in the hospital.

AFC AdamLondon

(Would rather be busting out a D20 on a Gargantuan Black Dragon and reaping the Vorpal Longsword, baby. Yeah!!!!)

As my success continued I acted more and more like the prize, and the more I did it the more attractive I became.

Not the suggested norm but.... (Not for those new to game): April 13, 2007

Ok guys,

Being the prize. We all know how important it is to get the girls number at the end of an interaction (or the middle if you really want it to work). However, have you ever considered how this makes you look in terms of being the prize?

I'm obviously talking about a minor difference. However imagine the strength of doing a set and then leaving your number and telling them to call you.

I've tried it twice.

So it's all still fresh, however as always I like to break it down for the forum as I go.

Yesterday I approach a young oriental HB7. I've been staring at her ass for the last 20 minutes as I'm shopping and decide I need to get it.

AFC AdamLondon: You're like me. Couldn't wait to eat today eh?

HB: Sorry?

AFC AdamLondon: Early lunch?

HB: Oh, yeah.

AFC AdamLondon: You don't work around here do you?

HB: No, I do.

AFC AdamLondon: Wow, I just I thought I was the only guy under 30 that worked around here. Everyone else is like 50+

HB: Hahaha, nah, I'm young. I work at UBS.

AFC AdamLondon: There you go, and I thought I was the only one. Looks like there is a chance for me to do lunch with someone who isn't greying then.

HB: Yeah that'd be nice.

AFC AdamLondon: Here's my card. Email me and we'll arrange.

HB: Thanks will do.

Then I received this.

Hi Adam,

Just wanted to say Hi! You did make me laugh yesterday... funny how you think everyone in Mayfair is over 50!

Anyway...would be good to do lunch sometime (with someone who isn't an OAP). Girls and guys gotta eat.

Get back when you can,

Jen

I think this is a stronger frame as I wasn't to fussed about whether she contacted me or not, which kind of gets her to do the chasing a little earlier.

Still analysing, but would love others input.

AFC AdamLondon - Always Learning

Then I got the replies...I suppose I should be more careful who I chat to.

Re: Not the suggested norm but.... (Not for those new to game): April 13, 2007

The girl and I have been texting back and forth. We set up a lunch date and I asked her to tell me something interesting about herself. You will never believe the reply. Yeah... sounds good for a first lunch. Well an interesting fact about me is that my uncle is Jackie Chan. Seriously. Jen

Forget her! I wanna meet her uncle!

I will gladly admit that my frame has been entirely destroyed! Jackie Chan is like a legend! He's my hero! Man I love this chick!

Ok, now I just realised that she is Jade from the cartoon Jackie Chan Adventures and sent her a quick cartoon image of herself.

HAHAHA

Ok this isn't even game anymore, it's just fun. So awesome though, without the community I'd never have met her.

And never have learnt of Jackie Chan if I hadn't used, "Tell me something interesting about yourself."

The power of game!!!

AFC AdamLondon

Re: Motorbikes?: April 17, 2007

I bought a Vespa about 3 weeks ago.

It's amazing.

I live in central and work here. It's almost impossible to go faster than 30 mph due to speed restrictions and traffic, though my little baby can hit 60.

The girls love it. A lot of my female friends hang out with footballers who have super-bikes and/or Ferrari's. Yet they all prefer to sit on the back of my lil red Vespa. Catnap has got it right, it's the Italian suave thing in the city... nipping between traffic jams and scooting around.

AFC AdamLondon

Yet despite the constant work to make myself attractive, I still hadn't formalised my ideas. I wanted help.

Commercial Products, Let the People Speak! April 20, 2007

So I'm sitting at work and wondering:

The community is inundated with commercial outfits, each with it's own pro's and con's. Yet from what I can see, very little market research has been done as to what those already in the community would like to achieve, or what product they would like to see developed.

As you all know I spend a lot of my time analysing new theories, and breaking down what people do, to try and find the most efficient route to a woman's knickers. That's because I like being busy and the quicker I can do it, the more I can fit into a day. However there are also other angles. For example, I want to get higher and higher quality girls.

Anyway, I figure rather than working blindly and just randomly practising something and then not being focused, I'd do something that should have been done a long time ago.

What does the community want?

This is something I feel will help all commercial outfits, and ultimately the whole community, by giving us exactly what we want to learn.

So lets use this thread. Write down a list of the things you'd like to learn.

Everyone do it, and lets see if patterns emerge.

I'd like to learn how to game strippers quickly and take them home the night you meet them.

AFC AdamLondon

My bike was rapidly becoming an integral part of my game.

Getting Lucky? Luck = Preparation Meeting Opportunity: April 26, 2007

We are all aware of the phrase "getting lucky."

Well last night I made a decision that made me realise just how much that statement shouldn't apply to us.

Getting lucky implies that we have no control over the results... or little control at least. So the essence of game should remove this, right?

A good friend of mine described luck as preparation meeting opportunity. You can't capitalise on a "break" if you aren't ready for it.

example: HB comes over to sit with you (giving you proximity) yet your fear of approach stops you from talking to her. If you were prepared and had practised you would be able to start the conversation after recognising the IOI and get the girl.

However this runs deeper. How many of you have been in the game for a while, yet still go home empty handed? Are you missing something? Something other than IOI's or conversation hooks.

Are you prepared to get laid?

Last night I took my brand new Vespa, which I love, to Chinawhites. However, even though I was initially riding alone, I took a spare helmet. Why? This was a conscious choice I made before going to the club. I knew that if I didn't bring a spare helmet I couldn't take a girl home. I would have allowed myself to fail. I realised that subconsciously I was weighing up the decision to carry it.

A part of my mind was actually convincing me to leave it at home as it would be hassle to carry. On analysis I realised it was actually a form of AA. I was allowing myself to fail to get an f-close so that if I did well in a set and wasn't sure if I could get her home, I could always say to myself, "No point in trying to get her home, you only have one helmet."

So I made the decision and took it with me.

I played in the club. Chinas on Wednesday is one of my haunts.

I bumped into the PUA Training crowd; said hi but didn't really mingle with them as I wanted to do some lone stuff. I moved from table to table mingling with the groups of girls I am on pretty good terms with. The key for me here was to build up masses of social proof without my own table. So I was using contacts to get introduced to others.

It ended with me chatting to one Portuguese girl. As we go to leave the club she spots my second helmet.

HB: Hey, you didn't tell me you had two helmets! You can ride me home.

AFC AdamLondon: Oh man... I can't be arsed.

HB: Oh, come on... We've danced and chatted all night, it's the proper thing to do.

AFC AdamLondon: Oh man I really don't want to

HB: Come on you're taking me home.

AFC AdamLondon: Where do you live?

HB: White City

AFC AdamLondon: Oh no, man. That really is far. Seriously, I don't want to, another night.

HB: Come on... Show me your bike, be a gentleman.

AFC AdamLondon: Ok babe. Fair enough I'll take you

So now I ask you to stop reading and think. Whose frame is this? Am I in hers? Or is she in mine? (mwahahahahahaha)

So we get on my bike. She negs me for poor driving, I tell her she's wrong and that she is drunk and so thinks the road is swerving.

And we ride... To my house! ☺

HB: Where are we?

AFC AdamLondon: My house.

HB: Why?

AFC AdamLondon: I'm tired

HB: I thought you were taking me home.

AFC AdamLondon: I am... in the morning. I need my sleep first.

In we go, we get to bed, we cuddle. We don't sleep. We kiss. We f-close.

Now the key here is that I couldn't have done it if I had allowed myself to fail by not bringing the helmet, which ultimately got me the lay.

So beware. Be prepared. Have condoms, plan to come home with someone, have the logistics taken care of. You will increase the chances of it happening if you do.

There are a lot of community guys I know that don't prepare. They aren't sure where or how they will take a girl home to f-close her. Read HumJobs thread. This guy was my first wing and a really good PUA. However, when we sat down we realised he didn't have a plan on how he was actually going to Lay the girl.

From when we planned it, it took him like a week or so. Plan yours. How will you close them? Where?

Are you ready for success?

AFC AdamLondon

HB Persia Entourage Game - Direct - Sex School: May 01, 2007

Hey Guys,

This is more for me than anything else. It's one of those landmark points in my journey of game. I woke up this morning in the bed of the Persian girl I met on Friday night. I want to run through the entire interaction as there are a lot of points I felt are useful to learn from, for myself to re-read in the future and for others to see if they can use.

So I meet this girl at Paper last Friday. We brought 78 women with us that night, it was hectic. If you want to know how run off my feet I was, ask Beckster, he saw.

Anyway, I saw this girl and she stood out from the others, mostly because all the others are happy to flirt and dance on the table, but this girl wasn't interested. She was happy to just dance with one of her friends off the table as we couldn't fit everyone on. Her lack of neediness was definitely attractive. I didn't really see her for the bulk of the night. I spent a lot of time flirting with the girls on our table and the other tables around. I then move off the table to get a breather and I see HBPersia and HBfriend standing in the bar area. I move over to them and do a dance with them both. HBPersia pulls my jacket off, and I continue to grind with them both. I then move towards HBPersia ignoring the other girl and pull her into me. Grinding hard and placing our foreheads together. We are almost about to kiss. I pull away, and head back to my group.

I stop and ask her if she fancies coming to the park the following day for a picnic? She agrees, and I move off.

I then ignore her for most of the night. I do random things like pouring alcohol down the necks of strange girls, or going into the VIP area with some random chick. Unknown to me HBPersian sees this.

I go back to the two of them and she blanks me. I persist. I pull her to me and flirt with her friend. Her friend is more than amicable, yet Persia keeps pushing me away.

With an hour to go, HB Persia says goodbye to Jim Stark and then leaves to go.

AFC AdamLondon: Wait!

HB Persia begins to run. So I chase. I catch her on the stairs and pull her into me.

AFC AdamLondon: So 12 tomorrow?

HBPersia: Maybe.

AFC AdamLondon: It's hard to arrange a meet-up on a maybe.
HBPersia: We'll see.

AFC AdamLondon: I thought you were the spontaneous type.

HBPersia: I am.

AFC AdamLondon: Good, what's the best way to get in contact with you?

HBPersia: I don't know.

AFC AdamLondon: What's your number? (Pull out my phone)

HBPersia: I'm not giving you my number.

AFC AdamLondon: It's going to be hard to get in contact with you if you don't give it to me.

HBPersia: Be inventive... if you want it, work it out.

AFC AdamLondon: What?

HBPersia: You're a clever boy. Get in touch.

With that she leaves.

So I'm thinking, OK, whatever. I stay at the club for a bit then leave to go to an after party and close a blonde.

I awake the next day at 9:30 a.m... God knows why. And text Jim.

Adam: Dude, I need the number of the hot Persian girl from the model agency last night.

Jim: Which one?

After 30 minutes of trying to remember her name, we crack it (I owe you one Jim!). I text her.

"Hey cutie, so random meeting you last night. See you at 12 p.m, Marble Arch. Don't be late!"

I get the response

HB: Can we make it 1 p.m?

So it's on.

We meet at the park. And now I'm on my day 2 game. Essentially this basically means treat her as if you've known her forever. I grab her arm to link up. She pulls away. I do it again. She pulls away.

HBPersia: Why are you holding my arm?

AFC AdamLondon: I don't want to lose you

HBPersia: You won't.

AFC AdamLondon: I might, you are very small.

HBPersia: Small?

AFC AdamLondon: Yeah, I could lose you in the crowds.Link arms and lock. Hook line and sinker!

We spend the first part of the day on the row boats. I used to row in school so it is a bit of a DHV, especially when the other guys on the river can't do it. We then get off and go to the Diana Memorial and chill in the park. I lie down, I put her head on my arm. I kiss her forehead.

If you learn nothing else from me ever, learn this:ON A DAY 2, KISS HER FOREHEAD! OFTEN!

I have asked the princesses about this and they all agree. It is one of the most attractive things you can do on a day 2. Naturals do it from time to time, especially the older ones with younger girls. It works. Try it.

I then kiss her neck, her ear, and finally we go to kiss. I pull away and keep building up her buying temperature.

Cut a long story short... She starts grinding on me.

AFC AdamLondon: Ahem.

HBPersia: Mmmm, yes baby?

AFC AdamLondon: Kids

HBPersia: What?

AFC AdamLondon: Look.

And right there staring at us are a bunch of 8 year olds with their mouths wide open.

Oops. She gets incredibly embarrassed. I ask her if she'd like to move somewhere more private, we do.

From here on in it's simple. Kiss, stroke, kiss neck, stroke. We are in a quiet bit in the park and basically bring each other off with our hands and mouths. It's hot, she's hot. I love game.

We leave and get on my Vespa! She says, "Wow I love it! It's so European. I think you're soo sexy." She grabs my nuts.

I think its the best £1300 I ever spent.

We go to dinner and pass Amora. We set up the next date to go there on Monday. It's our sex date.

Then she goes home and I get a lovely text.

"I'm amazed I've met someone like you, Adam. Not only are you amazing, but you understand females. That's one in a million. See you at 9 for our sex date."

That text was a direct result from being in the community, and with a little help from my princesses.. Thank you all!

Last night we went to Amora. Check out the upcoming review of that FUCKING AWESOME day 2 location.

(Hint... in the orgasm tunnel you can get behind the display and take her top off and then dry-fuck a girl up the wall. No cameras. None that we saw anyway)

Kino escalation is easy there. Anyway I bought some massage oil from the shop and it was on. I told her my place was messy and that it wouldn't be right there. And I wanted to see how she lived. We went back to her place.

I then jumped on her computer and found her modeling pictures. Up until now only Jim had seen them.

I stay at her place, we have an incredible night and then wake up in the morning and get on a train together to come to town. I'm still in the clothes I wore yesterday as I write this at my computer at work.

Points to note.

With extreme social proof you need to be sure you generate comfort

Persistence works

On a day 2 get them to link arms with you instantly

Kiss her forehead

LeadGo to sex academies

Love the game

Play Dungeons and Dragons

I hope this helps, as usual, any questions just ask.

AFC AdamLondon

Sometimes I was pushing things so fast the girls were getting buyers remorse.

ASD - Anti Slut Defence: May 02, 2007

Ok Guys,

As you know I'm always up for escalating my game and I've

now found something I'm not sure is talked about very often. ASD or Anti Slut Defense. This is what appears to happen if you escalate to a close too quickly.

Now I'm really not one for one night stands. I like to see a girl regularly and have her in my life. However recently I've been experimenting with escalated kino to close at an incredible pace. It has happened in 2 hours in some situations.

I then get the most unbelievable responses the next day. LMR of an incredible note. These girls will suddenly stop responding to my texts or calls, become incredibly emotional or even rude. I had one girl turn up to a day 4 (the close was on the day2) with a friend. It was as if it was a first meeting all over again.

Be warned, escalating too quickly can ultimately give you too much work to deal with in the future. If you're after a ONS then it doesn't matter.

Hope this helps.

AFC AdamLondon

After the Persian girl I managed to close a gorgeous Greek lady, which prompted me to write the following.

---

300 The Movie Close! - Sort of - God I'm a Geek: May 03, 2007

Hey guys,

This is not a lay report but it still amused me.

What do the battle of Thermopylae and AFC AdamLondon have in common? Read on!

Last night I K-Closed a stunning chick!

And....

Wait for it.....

She's GREEK!!!!

That means I have a Greek and a Persian Fighting over me! Just like Thermopylae.

Ahahahahahahahahahahahahahahaha

I'm a geek.

AFC AdamLondon

Then the Newspapers in London started noticing me. I' d had a few pieces before, but I was appearing in something almost every other week.

Re: I'm in the London Paper Today: May 10, 2007

Cheers for support and messages I have gotten about being in the paper.

Sorry I haven't mentioned much about it here, it's just that with so many commercial adverts being plugged on the forum I figured they hardly needed one more. I prefer giving everything I have material wise away for free, and then helping individuals improve themselves via the one-to-one's.

I took the newspaper to Chinawhites last night to give to one of my friends. Some HB saw it and she's like...

HB: Wow, so you're famous huh?

AFC AdamLondon: Hardly. You would think a guy that teaches people how to get girls can pull. Yet somehow I just can't manage it.

HB: You're not shy of girls, right?

AFC AdamLondon: Nope... but I just can't seem to find someone I click with. Have you seen the other dance floor?

HB: Nope.

AFC AdamLondon: Come with me.

Mwahahahahahahaha Close!

I will use any opportunity to steal a moment. Hey, I might never be in the paper again.

AFC AdamLondon

Though the easier it became to close them the more difficult the situations I'd find myself in.

Reading the signs... How women communicate without words: May 10, 2007

Hey guys,

I've k-closed this girl twice over the last few weeks, but every time I try and sort out a day 2, she refuses. It's not in a bad way, just in a "sorry, I can't make it" way.

Now, with me not being the kind to chase and her knocking back the ones I suggest, it just hasn't happened.

Then it occurs to me....

I send a text.

Adam: Hey cutie. You know, you are the hardest person to take on a date. This leads me to believe that either a) you have a boyfriend or b) you only want me for my body."

HB: Hahahah, actually I do have a) but that doesn't stop me wanting b).

This of course leaves me in a difficult dilemma as it means I've kissed someone in a relationship, which is something that really goes against what I do. Naturally, I've cut things off.

However it's amazing to note that if you just read in between the lines it's easy to see what's going on. How easy would it have been for me to just pretend I hadn't noticed something going on and to let her carry on her game.

Sometimes not acting is worse than initiating a problem.

My two cents.

AFC AdamLondon

The more attractive I became the easier it became to be comfortable being me. It was like a positive cycle with every success driving me onwards and to better positions.

I am a Geek. I am Proud: May 12, 2007

If I've learnt anything about game it's about being happy being yourself.

People will often tell you, "Getting girls is easy, just be yourself."

The simple fact is, many people are shy about who they really are. They feel uncomfortable expressing themselves in the way they wish to be seen. They often over compensate for weaknesses and try to impress the girl, or are shy and withdrawn.

I am a geek. A geek and proud. Right now I am on my way home from a three hour journey to a prop making company where I have just spent a good deal of money on a suit of armour so I can go live role playing. I am trying to decide what to do with my day tomorrow, between meeting up with a ballet dancer I met last night, Jackie Chan's niece or sword fighting in a cave in my new armour.

Will I hide my nature as a geek to girls? Hell no! I just bought armour from the movie *Troy*! It looks amazing. I found out me and Brad Pitt have the same size head (DHV). These are all interesting facts about me, based on my geekdom. As long as you are happy with yourself and your pastimes and you don't let them take over your life or present them in a weird and over excited way, you will probably find most girls are more than willing to accept you for who you are.

Be yourself, be happy being yourself. Be your best self.

AFC AdamLondon

HBMixedRace - Tried a new routine: May 14, 2007

So Wednesday I'm partying at Chinawhites when I see this girl and I am literally breathless. I have a real weakness for mixed race girls after a NY chick I met in my pre-game days.

Anyway, she is hanging around this big bruiser of a rudeboy, a big, muscular, Jamaican looking type. As she has a boyfriend I pretty much ignore her and spend my time dancing on the tables with my girls. After a while I notice her giving me IOI's. I move over to say hi, and we start dancing.

I back off a bit as she has a BF, and I won't cross the boundary.

Suddenly she comes towards me and is like, "By the way, that guy is just my friend. I'm single."

All I can think is OMGFG (that's Oh My Good Fucking God!).

So we dance, and I begin kino escalation. Basically just dry fucking her through my clothes. I ask her if she's seen the R&B room, and move her through to there.

1) So I can have a legitimate reason to grind

2) To isolate.

Man I love Chinawhites.

Anyway, I then decide to try a bit of a routine a friend of mine has worked on. I rarely use routines and figured it'd be worth it.

Looking back I can't believe I was gonna risk it on a girl I value so highly but, meh. Thats what game does to you.

AFC AdamLondon: On a scale of 1 to 10, how comfortable do you have to be with someone before you kiss them?

HBMixedRace: 11.

AFC AdamLondon: Interesting. And where do I currently rate on that scale?

HBMixedRace: 3.

AFC AdamLondon: Ok then... looks like we have some work to do.

We continue dancing. We laugh.

I organise a day 2 out to dinner (incidentally that restaurant was mentioned in thelondonpaper as a quaint little restaurant but no good for a first date. Me and many HB's disagree).

I number close to arrange the date properly.

AFC AdamLondon: On a scale of 1 to 10 where do I now rate?

HBMixed Race: 7.

AFC AdamLondon: Interesting.

I leave and days go by. Saturday we meet for the date. I do my usual by treating her as a girlfriend on the date. She is really responding. I then take us into Cafe de Paris.

I had to organise Bullboy, Mega Mike, and Beckster entry to the club that night, as well as another 15 students of mine and then there were the usual faces, including one of my instructors who is a magician at the club.

Slowly but surely everyone comes to say hello.

HBMixedRace: You know like everyone in London.

AFC AdamLondon: I really don't... Hey Lizzie!

HBMixedRace: See!

AFC AdamLondon: Nah, she's just a friend.

Beckster: Hey Adam!

HBMixedRace gives me the *help, I'm caught in a social proof trap and I'm gonna sleep with you* look.

Anyway, the night goes on and I kind of ignore her verbally while stroking her ass as I talk to everyone else around us.

We move to the dance floor.

AFC AdamLondon: On a scale of 1 to 10, where am I?

HBMixedRace: I'm not sure.

AFC AdamLondon: Let's find out... K-Close

So the night goes on and I decide I'm getting tired, so we leave the club.

[Take note....it is important not just to read advice on the forum but to use it! STUPID MOTHER FUCKER FORGOT HIS SECOND EFFING BIKE HELMET!!!!!!!]

AFC AdamLondon: Hey babe, it's getting late. Why not crash at mine and get the train in the morning?

HBMixedRace: I'd love to.

AFC AdamLondon: Shit, I forgot my other helmet. It's OK, I'll get you a cab.

I pay the driver, give him my address, and get home.

The girl turns up and thankfully I've had the time to move my new Spartan live role play helmet off my bed.

We go to bed and I f-close.

AFC AdamLondon: You've just slept with a geek.

HBMixedRace: You too.

AFC AdamLondon: No, I mean it.

Then I reach over and show her my latest purchase. (See picture below)

She laughs and then an idea comes to me. You see this girl has an amazing body, six pack and everything. Suddenly I tell her to put the helmet on.

I kid you not. She gets up, perfect breasts perky in front of her, wearing my bloody Greek helmet. I think I have a new fetish!

Anyway, she's a cool chick and I'm now off to meet her for dinner.

It was a pretty good routine to use, maybe try experimenting with it. It's kind of direct, kind of leading.

AFC AdamLondon

The forum was about a lot more than just a chance to learn how to game girls. We offered each other advice on everything. When one of my friends was looking for the push to leave his job, I made sure to help him.

The point is that becoming attractive is about working on all aspects of your life, not just the funny things you say. As I was improving I was learning this. Every aspect of my life was helping me to improve.

Re: Decisions: May 18, 2007

Leave your job.

I've run lots of small businesses. I've been homeless. I've lived in foreign countries. I've lost almost all my family. I've been fired, I've been stabbed, I've been told my leg may have to be amputated, I've contracted some serious diseases, I've had a face off with a green mamba, I've lost thousands of pounds.

Yet each of those things was an experience I would never ever regret. They were just the down points. The highs... well lets just say they were amazing.

If you don't do it, you will always be saying, "What if?"

It may fall apart but building it up again is the best part. Yeah, it's been a hell of a ride, and is far from over.

Everyone tells me I'm lucky. I say luck is preparation meeting opportunity. Whenever anything arises.. I run for it full pelt!

I try anything once, and sometimes keep trying it. I want to be successful. I just won't do it by hurting others. It isn't easy, it takes time, and I may fail. But what a journey, eh?

If nothing else, when I first started in game I had things to talk about – my life. The fact that I have done more things in the last five years than most people do in 30 is one hell of a conversation topic.

Live life to the full. Do it, I'm with you! If it all goes tits up you can crash on my floor.

AFC AdamLondon

Being Responsible - Important - Please Read: May 23, 2007

Hey guys,

I was out last night with three wings, and about ten girls. It was the launch party of Amora. We all had a great time looking at all the sex toys, spanking each other and networking like bitches.

We then headed off to the after party at Chinawhites. One of our girls didn't look so good and as the night went on, she looked worse still.

I handed her to one of our guys to watch and maybe look into getting her home, as they get on well. I notice they are gone. Suddenly my mate comes to find me. She's collapsed and not in a good way. I go upstairs to find her in the street barely able to hold her head up. I hold her in my arms, her body is completely limp.

Security call us a cab and direct it to take us to UCL hospital. I tell the two guys to come with me, as I don't think it's clever to be left alone with her. In the cab she leans against me, I try to keep her awake. Suddenly she looks at me and freaks out.

"Who are you? What are you doing to me?"

She looks to her right and sees the other guy.

"I'm scared, what's going on?"

We talk to her and try to calm her down.. she lapses into unconsciousness again.

We wake her once more. She relaxes, she starts frothing at the mouth. She cries.

At this point I have one of those *shit, what am I doing?* moments.

She freaks out and believes we took advantage of her. I think over what I've done. We always had more than one person present with her, got her water, kept her safe. Still I weigh up the evidence of a girl out of her mind, and what she could say. Then my defence being myself and 2 other guys, all part of a seduction community.

How much are we likely to be believed???

We make sure the cabbie takes us direct to the hospital, at least that way he can vouch for us. I forget to get his details....

We get her inside, she sobers up. She gets looked over. There are no traces of any drugs, just a bad case of drunk and disorderly.

The key fact here is that not getting the cabbies number was a mistake; he was my one real witness that we took her directy to the hospital. Other than that I think I played it safe. But then again I wasn't drinking and was thinking clearly, trying to keep in mind what could happen if I didn't cover all angles.

If any of us ever found ourselves accused of something and the community came to light, it would go against us in a big way. We have to all be incredibly responsible in these matters and try to be overly careful when it comes to looking after our fairer sex.

Have fun. Be safe.

AFC AdamLondon

By now there was a change in the way people ran game. There were arguments as to whether it was better to concentrate on building up your life or learning routines and running game. This debate would last for ages. Naturally I wanted to join in, as I felt I'd worked on both.

The Missing Link - Routines or not routines? That is the question!:

Hey Guys,

As you know, I love experimenting with new ideas, reading through old ones, and re-analysing them. With this in mind I had been inspired by the influx of recent posts concerning routines.

Should you use them? Or should you go direct or be natural?

If any of you look over my first posts when I joined the forum, you will see I was very much anti routines. I would specifically use AFC style questions, but worded and presented in a way that still enabled me to close. However as I have taught more and more I have learnt that routines definitely have their place in game.

Notably they are as a means to teach those new to the game who may not have the confidence, experience or even just the knowledge of what to say.

So I begun by developing set routines people could use to get started. Then I'd try to pull them away from the routines as quick as possible. There is, however, a serious point to be made here, one that is even a key part of real MM training.

Your routines are not supposed to be rehearsed lines repeated throughout the community with everyone saying the same thing.

They are more than that. They should be personal.

Now, whether you decide to create a personal routine to build up a specific stage in MM or whether you just want a conversation piece as a filler while going direct, I don't think it particularly matters.

However it wouldn't hurt those of you currently using *who lies more* and the *jealous girlfriend opener* to build up your own stack based on your own lives.

So this post is really aimed at those of you with some standing in game who are looking to make that move towards something a little more natural. Allow your own personality to shine through and make a step towards "being yourself." This is something a lot of people will tell you is the best way to attract a girl.

At this point I can almost hear a chorus of people saying their life is boring and they have nothing to say about it, or what routine about my life should I be saying and how do I say it?

I would start with picking up a pen and paper and writing a few things down. You can start out structured, however be sure to throw this paper away. It is not a "cheat sheet" nor are your life routines something that should be scripted or remembered and presented in a certain order. Rather you are identifying key interesting moments in your life that you can share with someone else as time goes by.

Feel free to open however you wish. However, if you want to use an opinion opener why not use one that actually relates to you?

"Can I just ask you a quick opinion? Should I get the cheese and tomato or the beef?"

"Can I just ask you a quick opinion? I'd love an outsiders view on this point; should I quit my job of five years for a new one with better prospects but more risk?"

Whatever the opener, if it genuinely is related to your life you will find it easier to build conversation.

Have you ever wondered why it is hard to build conversation after, "Does my t-shirt make me look gay?" The reason is that you genuinely have no connection with that routine. Unless, of course, you really do think it makes you look gay. In which case maybe the opener might be better off being "Do you have any idea why I'm wearing this t-shirt that makes me look gay?"

So you're in. Hopefully by now you should be having some form of natural, genuine conversation about the topic.

You may be looking for something to talk about. Why not ask one open-ended question? Remember, you've never met this person, you could ask absolutely anything. From a game point of view it may be better to ask something that really makes her think. Something like;

"Ok cutie, here's one for you. What's your passion in life?" or "What's the most interesting thing that's ever happened to you"

This is designed to really open them up and to relieve the pressure from you of having to actually think of what to say. You can be thinking about where you stand while she is thinking of what to say.

From here the conversation should go a lot more natural, and this is where your natural routines or "life routines" should really begin to be used.

So what are they?

Well think back to 4 or 5 key events in your life, some good, some bad.

1) I used to live in (a) but now I live in (b). Its amazing how different life is between the two, yadda yadda (bonus points if you use yadda yadda in set).

2) Well I currently work as (a) which I kind of fell into, because when I grew up I wanted to be a (...).

3) I was hoping to go to (...) on holiday last year however my (gran/aunt/cousin/dog) got really ill, so I wanted to be there to look after them....

4) Personally, I don't understand why so many people allow their relationships to get so bad. Me and my last girlfriend....

5) Do you do sports? What one? Wow, I actually play (....). I didn't think I'd like it and just joined but once you try it, it's awesome. Seriously you should give it ago, once I....

I mean this is just a sample of things. I've tried to think of some basic topics and hopefully everyone should relate to at least one. Elaborate on these and think of your own 4 or 5. Put them into words.

Then burn it!

Remember, the key thing about this is that these are real memories. You can remember little factors like how the wind felt or whether your parents were there. These added details build up the story and let others relate to it. This is the key to engaging someone and making yourself sound interesting.

Use this as a stepping-stone to move off of conventional canned material and towards a more natural conversation.

Give it a try. What have you got to lose?

As always, if there are any questions just give me a PM.

AFC AdamLondon

Re: Time Required for a Solid Number Close - According to Sinn: May 24, 2007

I think the difference between those that succeed regularly and those that don't is the understanding that your life has to consist of something other than game.

You need attractive qualities, which build a foundation with which you can proceed. Qualifying statements, NLP, routines, all only add a small percentage to your chance of success with the much larger part being based on confidence, looking after yourself, having ambition etc.

As Skeletor has mentioned, to improve these aspects take time. You will have to really want to improve and put some time and effort into it. I've paid a lot of money to get straight teeth. Could I game before? Hell yes. Has my game improved since? Hell yes. That is an aspect that wouldn't have improved if I didn't do it.

That is a percentage that would have been missing. I could have got up to 95% (for arguments sake) but I would always have been missing that final piece.

It isn't necessary for us to get 100% but it is important to understand that the more pieces of the puzzle you collect the easier it becomes.

Look at the guys from PUA Training (sorry to pick you guys out, it's just you have photos on your site). Check out their Web site. They all do well with girls. Spot the unfashionable one that doesn't look good. Oh wait... there isn't one. Do they have game? The ones I've met definitely do. Would they do as well if they didn't have those polished looks and smart clothes? Maybe...

The point is, their game is increased by making themselves as attractive as they can, pre-game. This includes everything, from confidence, which can be helped with tapping, or taking a sport which can help with dance. It goes right through to learning how to converse properly, with my new up and coming e-book, *Conversation - An Art or a Hindrance?* (just kidding)

The fact is there are a number of aspects to work on. Find which method suits you, but whatever method you choose, remember that a much much larger piece of the pie is taken up with these other aspects.

Have you all seen the images of Style when he did the stand up comedy pre-game and how he looks now? Coincidence? Think about that.

AFC AdamLondon

....

My Method

I'd almost been gaming for a year and in that time I'd had a massive change in my perceptions towards what was possible. I taught people from all over the world and transformed them from being shy geeks with no hope with women, to absolute babe magnets capable of getting whoever they wanted. I had never really come to terms with my driving force. I didn't know what really wanted me to succeed.

Principles of Attraction

This post started with the title *Unbelievable, after 1 year she still has me - Life Fuck Up Report*, but I've changed it as I wrote down everything I went through and all the mistakes I made. I realised I AM a different person and the feelings that washed over me causing me to write this post have all but disappeared as I wrote it. I may not be the best at game, I may not even be a PUA, but fuck me, I have had a lot of women, and I understand how to make them want me.

Almost 1 Year - Life Fuck Up Report: May 24, 2007

I know this is traditionally supposed to be written on my 1 year anniversary but I'm saving all the good points for that. This is why I got into game....

So I have been in the game for almost a year. I joined after breaking up with my girlfriend. For those that don't know, here's the story.

I met this girl in KFC in Plaza shopping centre. I was currently dating a girl but it wasn't going well.

HBPhilipino: Why are you eating alone?

The Real AFC Adam: Because I'm a sad loner with no mates,

what's your excuse?

HBPhilipino: I'm waiting for a friend.

The Real AFC Adam: Yeah right.

HBPhilipino: Seriously.

The Real AFC Adam: Ok, fair enough. I'm Adam. (Extends hand)

HBPhilipino: I'm Amanda

We fluff talk, her friend arrives and she disappears, but not before handing me a business card and saying, "Don't do lunch alone again."

Now check me, I knew what to do about this. I waited... 7 days. Most people tell you to wait for two days so I waited 7 to really maximise the effect.

Ahem

So I call her, "Hey babe, fancy lunch tomorrow?" She accepts and off we go.

Looking back I was actually really funny on the date. I kept negging the waitress and taking the piss out of her behind her back, while giving sly glances to my date.

We both explained how we were seeing other partners and agreed to be friends.

Friends that spent the next month spending every day and night together. I lived close to her work, so it made sense to sleep over. Obviously we didn't kiss or have sex... Hell, that would have moved things too quickly. So a month passes, and then we kiss. I know the correct thing to do.

The next day I dump my girlfriend. We hadn't got on well for months, I had hardly seen her because I was busy with work or something. Oh no, wait, I was busy with my new "friend."

Anyway, for my birthday my new friend bought me a lollipop

and a ticket to Germany to go for a week holiday with her. Three days after dumping my girlfriend I asked her out with a bunch of flowers and a card that said, "Will you be my girlfriend?"

Then she popped it out to me. She was an avid Christian and to be with her I'd have to convert.

So disappeared my life. I spent 2 nights a week studying to be a Christian, the rest working on my PR company.

I would wake up with her every morning and walk her to work. When she got to work I would go to a little place near her office to buy breakfast and then bring it to her at her desk. Then I would go home and work before going back and meeting her for lunch. Then I would go home and work before going out to meet her at the end of the day and walk her home.

On the 15th of every month I bought her flowers and a card with a new poem declaring my love.

Between this I worked...Hard.

However, she didn't like my choice of work assistant. A cute Malaysian girl who was an old friend of mine. So I dropped her. The work begun to overload, I stopped making new sales, the business fell apart. I needed money.

I confided in my girl friends. She didn't approve.

I dropped them.

I got frustrated with her one day. I wrote an email to a girl friend explaining this. She found it and I lied telling her my friend wrote it as he didn't like her.

She phoned my friend and I lost contact with him.

I got a new job in property. I started making a lot of money and I started working even more. I no longer had a single night free.

I fought back. I set up a Dungeons and Dragons night; one night a week where I would spend the evening playing with my mates.

She would cause fights all the way through it. I never had one night from start to finish without ruining it by being stuck in another room arguing with her.

She started getting angry all the time. Everything I did caused an argument. I wanted to spend more and more time away from her. Though the little free time I had outside of work was taken up with church studies or her.

I had no friends, I had no life. I did the only thing I could. I quit my job.

I got back into PR. I got social again. I found MSN at work. I regained my confidence flirting with girls online. They were old friends, girls I'd never closed but who had flirted with me as I was "safe."

I came home one night. I dumped her. I cried. A lot.

I called a friend over, the one who hated her. I wanted to commit suicide. I didn't tell him, he knew. He made a joke and told me to do it the following day. He's a good friend.

I went out clubbing, I met a girl. I had social proof from a natural friend of mine. Without knowing game I performed a camera opener, time constraint and befriended her friends before isolating and number closing.

A friend of mine recommended a book by a guy called Neil Strauss. I started reading it.

I met my ex for lunch.

She had been partying with Pharrell Williams. He took her number. She spent the entire lunch chatting to other guys in front of me.

I went home and cried.

I went out the following night with the new girl I k-closed and then left the club with a few mates, singing loudly with one girl in each arm! I kissed them both on the cheek.

I felt a tap on my shoulder. I turn around and there is my ex.

HBPhilipino: So this is why we broke up eh?

Not so AFC Adam: Hey babe, these are my new friends. This is Tracey and this is Annabel.

HBPhilipino: ... (She stormed off)

The following Saturday, I'm due to meet my new girl for lunch. I arrive when suddenly my phone rings.

AMOG Scott: Hey mate, there's a problem

Soon to be real AFC Adam: What's up buddy?

AMOG Scott: She had your keys... I couldn't stop them... they took everything.

She raided my flat and took everything, from PC to TV, from table to condoms. She rinsed me out. I called her; she picked up the phone and laughed.

I tried to reason with her. She laughed and hung up.

I told the new girl about game... I told her I had to learn, I had to understand it all. No woman would ever have that control over me again.

Yet every time my ex emailed me my heart jumped. I got fearful as to what she had wrote.

3 days ago I wrote to her.

Look this will be my last email to you. You are either ignoring me or have changed your email address and phone number. If you read this then at least send me a message telling me we won't speak again, in which case no hard feelings at least I can move on.

She replied just before I wrote this post.

Heya Babe,

I'm well. Sorry I didn't reply to your phone text about your missing stuff, I've been busy over the last few months. I'm in America at the moment for a friend's wedding, however I'll get back in touch when I come back to crappy London.

When I saw her name I freaked out, I didn't know what to do.

Now I've written this post I know exactly what to do.

I deposited so much time into being with her I confused it for love. The things I loved about her were mostly idolised images. They were ideals I placed on her that weren't really there. The more effort I put in, the more I wanted out and the less I got the more I wanted.

I think writing this post has actually helped me clarify things in my head.

Damn, I had no idea it would help that much. I really love you guys. I love this community. Whatever happens. Thank you.

AFC AdamLondon

After this I decided I wanted to break down my core principles into some kind of concise writing. Something that people could use to duplicate what I did.

It wasn't as easy as I'd hoped.

Breakdown of Language - The Meaning Behind Our Words and Interactions: May 30, 2007

Ok Guys,

This is an ongoing project of mine. However, rather than wait for the finished product, I thought I'd share with you what I have so far.

A lot of it is still jumbled in my head, so please excuse me if the explanations aren't as good as they should be. However I'll hope to clear this up if there are any questions.

Influencing behaviour through language

Ok, we've spoken a lot on here recently about the idea of routines and naturalism. However there is a middle ground here. I'm not talking about routines in any sense of the word rather I'm talking about being able to freestyle your speech in a way that directly influences the outcome of your target.

There are some core principles that govern our behaviour. Now bear in mind that these principles DO NOT apply to everyone. There are exceptions, however. You will probably find most people fit into these categories one way or another. If something doesn't work one way, then simply re-calibrate what you are saying and re-frame it to fit. Then continue as normal.

Before reading this, there is something I want you to bear in mind. As the wise words of Peter Parker once said, "With great power comes great responsibility." Don't abuse this! The idea behind this is that you will use it to leave people in a better state than when you found them.

There is an easier path, one where you could use these ideas to really convince a girl that you love her and that she loves you; then you will go and break her heart. Read through the posts that explain how to sleep with a girl without upsetting her. The principle applies. It may take a little more effort, but it's worth it.

Core Principles

1) We all want to be accepted

We are all concerned of others opinions of ourselves

2) We all (ultimately) want to be seen as being good

3) We all like to believe we are different

Now there may be more of these, and I can already hear some of you thinking... but that doesn't apply to me. Again, remember, this is merely a blanket; one that covers almost everyone but leaves the odd toe sticking out the bottom getting cold. Whereas some may not apply to you, odds are most and if not all, do. If you are one of the few to whom this does not apply then don't think you are out of the water.

You see, if someone can identify that none of them apply for you but that the reverse is true they can then tailor the conversation that way, and simply reverse all the aims.

The simple fact is that once you have someone's type you can get them.

Is this being truthful? Are you pretending to be someone else to get the girl? NO! That isn't the aim. The idea is to understand the core elements behind our interactions that will allow those who are not so good at flirting or being spontaneous to mimic naturals or those with a more direct game which *flows* without using routines.

What I am talking about will sound a lot like C+F. However even C+F can be hit and miss. I'm talking about specifically calibrating the C+F to achieve a specific goal. Ideally this is without altering any of your core values and without misleading the target.

Sound complicated?

That's because it is. For thousands of years we have been doing this naturally, so hopefully after reading this you will find that everything slips into place and you were probably doing most of it without realising and therefore the whole thing becomes a lot easier.

Are you still with me? I hope so.

So lets start with the beginning of an interaction.

What should I say? Opinion opener? Direct? Lets look at this from a different perspective. I have opened literally thousands of girls. Scrolling through my phone book I can see at least 100 girls I closed before Christmas this year. These are girls I closed before I could use Entourage. I actually spent some time and asked almost all of them if they could remember what I said when I opened them.

The simple fact is that they could not. I think maybe only one or two could remember and even they weren't sure.

The opener is for you, not them. It is literally a way to break the ice.

Why do opinion openers work so well? Well, they enable you to bypass a woman's natural defense that says you are hitting on her. It is a question that has an open end and expects her to actually think of and elaborate on an answer. Using the word *why* as a follow up to whatever she says will undoubtedly continue the conversation even further and further ingrain you into the set.

This is because when you are asking someone's opinion you are giving them a genuine compliment. You are subtly implying that you value their input. On top of this you have spent some time with them, which hasn't been altogether unpleasant and therefore you have begun to show that you are an interesting guy.

The opinion doesn't matter, the fact is you stayed in set and were interesting. You also displayed a level of interest in them and lead, all of which are attractive qualities.

In fact, if we were to look at it fully we would see.

Opening = Confidence = Attraction

Question = Genuine Interest = Comfort

Maintaining time in set = Attraction + Comfort

And we all know that comfort and attraction ultimately build towards a close.

Though it actually doesn't matter what is said.

Lets analyse a situation of a random good looking guy.

Hot Body + Opener = Confidence = A great deal of attraction

Dancing/Quick Statement = Higher value = Attraction

Display of interest in the girl = Comfort

Again we have the same result just in a different more organic and natural way.

The key is that you are building attraction to generate her interest and then comfort so that she feels comfortable being attracted to you. Make sense?

I hope so... I've just realised how long this is going to end up. Ok let's see what you think about this. If you like it I'll break down more.

AFC AdamLondon

I suppose by now it looked like everything I did succeeded, but this simply wasn't the case. I probably learnt a lot more from the ones I didn't succeed on, although these were rapidly dwindling. There was one in particular that was worthy of writing down as it really illustrated to me the importance of not treating someone differently.

Messed Up: A Conscious Choice with a High Risk of Failure, Does What it Says on the Tin: June 06, 2007

Hey guys,

Game isn't all about succeeding. In fact, a good portion of it is about failure. So here is my most recent failure. In fact, throughout my entire time on this forum it is the first time I've been LJBF'd.

I meet this girl about 3 weeks ago on a Project Entourage night. I vibe with her, vibe with the others, ignore her for a bit and then continue dancing. One of our boys comes up to me.

Entourage Boy: "You know that girl?"

AFC AdamLondon: "The cute blonde? I do indeed"

Entourage Boy: "She can't be gamed"

The music in the room stopped. I turned my head to her and saw the most beautiful girl in the entire room. The focus shifted and zoomed in on her, as the rest of the room became a blur...

AFC AdamLondon: "Reeeaaallly? Hmmmmm..."

I approach, I dance, I kino, I lead. I ask her if she's seen the VIP area. I isolate, I kino escalate. Then a good friend of mine turns up and jumps all over me like a roving monkey.

I sense she is getting anxious to head back to her friends so I number close and plan dinner.

I continue vibing and after the night I text her.

AFC AdamLondon: Hey Cutie, so random meeting last night. Are you always so friendly to strangers?

HBBlonde: No, not often. Besides, you were friendly with everyone.

AFC AdamLondon: Yeah I know a lot of people, so lets go to that restaurant I told you about, when you free?

HBBlonde: I'm not often free. Besides, you have a lot of people you can take.

AFC AdamLondon: True but most of them don't interest me to the point where I would. Besides, I'm not asking anyone else. I'm asking you.

So she agrees. She comes along to a meal but unfortunately I have other friends there. It's just one of those things. We all go downstairs and party all night. I isolate, I k-close.

We keep kissing. My friend, her friend and the two of us head back to mine. We sleep in my bed and my friend and his girl sleep in the front room.

Now yes, I should have escalated. I should have done a lot but I was tired. I had work 3 hours later so I slept.

I bit her bum first.

Then she leaves. I try and arrange a meet up, but she's busy. Whatever, I play hard to get. She texts me and conveys interest. We meet again with two friends for ice cream and chats. Kino well, kiss on the lips but not snog (it's in public after all).

I decide I've had enough.

Guys, I've been running game for a long time. I'm tired of the chase. I figure rather than bother with all the shit, I'll cut through it.

Here's where I live up to my name.

AFC AdamLondon: Hey babe, you know what? I like you.

HBBlonde: Don't play a player.

AFC AdamLondon: You play all you like, I'm a professional. I charge for this shit.

HBBlonde: Hahaha.

AFC AdamLondon: Seriously though, I'm bored of games. I like you, I know you like me. Lets do dinner and see what happens.

HBBlonde: I'll let you know.

I get a text.

HBBlonde: Adam, no games. Just **L**etting you know, you really are an awesome guy (at least she didn't say cute). I really like you, it's **J**ust that I'm not gonna **B**e going there. Keep rocking and having **F**un though, yeah?

So there you have it. I stop playing the game for one minute, the first set in a year of hundreds of girls, and I get LJBF'd.

I told my flatmate, and she says it's coincidence.

What do you guys think? Is it over between me and her? From a personal point of view it is. Whether she wants me or not I'm not going there.

1) I'm too outcome dependent. Ironically this one was based on the initial interaction because of my friend's challenge (this is why most good guys on the forum won't demo on demand).

2) There is potential for me to get oneitis over her...and that ain't happening

3) My statement to her is I don't wanna do game. I'm sticking to my statement.

Either way I learnt more from that one set than I have from a lot of other more successful ones.

AFC AdamLondon

At this point, it would take more than just one minor mishap to affect my game.

Cambridge graduate, only one BF, is definitely not a slut... honest: June 14, 2007

So I don't normally do ONS's purely because I find them a little tacky and I prefer to MLTR the girl.

However, I haven't posted anything for a while and I thought this was a little entertaining. Sometimes it's better to just let things ride out.

I'm at 24 last Saturday night sitting there with the boys from Entourage. Social proof game is through the roof as ever and we are getting a lot of attention from the girls. We probably brought about 30 with us so it's not a massive night. But again all the girls were the hottest there by far.

In fact, I thought I'd try a cold approach as I hadn't done one for a few weeks. I see a cute pair of girls on the floor and as I go to approach I'm told that they are in fact with us.

Guys, if you haven't done it, seriously close girls as mates. Then use them to get others. It's single handedly the easiest way to do things.

Anyway, I'm listening to a few old students of mine who have done some Ross Jefferies stuff and one of them tells me about this new line he's been using.

HB: Are you gay?

Gay Looking PUA: No, I mean the idea of having a dick in my mouth just makes me feel sick. I couldn't understand why a woman would want to suck a dick and feel it get warm and hard in her mouth.

HB: OMG, it's the most amazing thing in the world...

I'm thinking... hang on, I can see that working...

So I approach one of the girls in the Entourage and try it on her. It works like a charm. I get bored. It's funny how when a line or routine works it can actually be a big turn off. Once you know you can close, why bother? I mean the hotties blur into each other. Unless of course there is a real challenge to be had still...

And here's where I get chatting to HBAsianBigTits. Funny enough she actually picked on me as I was teaching a student a few weeks back.

HBAsianBigTits: What do you do for a living?

AFC AdamLondon: Who me?

HBAsianBigTits: Yeah!

AFC AdamLondon: I run a relationship course.

HBAsianBigTits: I knew it, I saw you in the paper. You run that company... This is your student, you're hitting on my mate!

AFC AdamLondon: I can't believe you said that! I take one day off to go out with a good friend and suddenly I'm teaching him to hit on girls. Do you know how many friends I lose that way? Do I look dressed to meet women? Besides who works on a Saturday? Anyway I like your style, tell me something interesting about yourself.

I didn't close as I couldn't be bothered.

However it turns out one of our team did and she had come along to the party.

We get talking and a few things are apparent.

1) She is a Cambridge graduate in psychology

2) She doesn't fall for game

3) She is a professional type and has a placement in September

4) She has strict parents

5) She has big tits

6) She has only had one BF

7) She is falling for game

8) She has a size 6 waist

9) She doesn't do one night stands or random sex unless in a relationship

10) She has big tits.

I pretty much run comfort and kino escalation and she is ready to kiss. I feel her head bobbing towards mine and rubbing cheeks. We've held hands a few times, we've pulled away. A kiss is on the cards.

We use very few words. I prefer it that way. There is less chance for me to fuck things up so we're just sitting in silence rubbing each other's hands.

I hold off.

AFC AdamLondon: I need to tell you something.

HBAsianBigTits: What?

AFC AdamLondon: I break hearts.

HBAsianBigTits: OMG I knew it, I don't want to end up with a player.

AFC AdamLondon: I really think you're a cool girl and don't want to upset you, but I'm not after a relationship.

HBAsianBigTits: I don't want to get used, I don't do random sex.

AFC AdamLondon: I don't do random sex either. It's weird, I really like you but I know a relationship would just be too much.

HBAsianBigTits: We don't have to have a relationship.

AFC AdamLondon: What do you mean?

HBAsianBigTits: Well we could just, you know, have fun and then see what happens.

Obviously game doesn't work. Ahem.

I tell her I don't kiss at the table. I pull her to the toilets. We don't speak. I prefer it that way. Less chance for me to fuck things up. We head back to the table; time draws on. We all stand up to leave.

Her friend comes over and they start talking. Her friend obviously disapproves of me... it might have something to do with the conversation we had earlier about blowjobs and then me ignoring her. "Hey you can't talk to me about blowjobs and then just walk off" Apparently you can.

I don't interfere. I prefer it that way. Less chance for me to fuck things up.

She comes back to me and her friend leaves. We head back

to mine arm in arm and entertain small talk. We don't discuss where we are heading.

We get to my flat. I show her in but we don't discuss why we are there. We go to my room. We don't discuss why but she gets naked. Still there is no speech. I close.

I fall asleep with her in my arms.

We wake in the morning and she gets dressed. We have a little small talk but not too much. I prefer it that way; I like a quiet morning.

AFC AdamLondon

The pieces of the puzzle were finally coming together for me.

Follow the signs. They want to help you sleep with them: June 15, 2007

Hey guys,

As you know I'm always looking for new interesting parts of game. Something has caught my eye recently and I thought I'd bring to your attention.

I know we've had a lot of talks about *being yourself*, and self improvement. These are very important aspects, however they are still those moments where, unless you are an Adonis, you will get blown out. Language and humour are still key parts of game so I started trying to explain what my head does when I'm in set and try to explain the dynamics of language.

I started writing a post about the undercurrents of language but couldn't finish it as it wasn't clear in my head yet. However another piece has fit into place.

I think women tell you how to sleep with them, unconsciously. Check this.

PUA: Can I have your phone number?

HB: No, I don't give my phone number to strangers.

Looks like a blow out right? Wrong! A full knock back would be

HB: NO!

However she added erroneous conversation. In English we constantly abbreviate our words and language. We are inherently lazy creatures when it comes to communication.

How often do we shorten names and miss out letters in pronunciation? This is all natural to us. So why add additional information to the conversation unless it was placed there for you to use?

Lets take the earlier example.

HB: No, I don't give my phone number to strangers.

T*ranslation: If you weren't a stranger, you'd get my number*

So the aim then is to persist and reframe so that you are no longer a stranger.

I believe these keys are hidden throughout the whole interaction, you just have to find them. Shit tests definitely contain insights into these leads, as do other actions. Watch for them and follow the road.

AFC AdamLondon

....

Then an interesting turn of events happens. You see, the game is never really over. It just gets delayed for a while.

Re: Messed Up: A Conscious Choice with a High Risk of Failure, Does What it Says on the Tin: June 16, 2007

So I was in a terrible mood last night. Clubs were giving me trouble, some chode wanted a fight, I had an argument with my best friend and generally felt down. I've felt this way for a while...in fact since the girl in this thread. I sense oneitis.

After scouring the club and not seeing a single girl I liked, I left. As I walk out I bump into the HB and a friend (point to note: after reading back over the thread I didn't add any form of name after HB on this one. That was a subconscious choice...what does that say?).

HB: Where are you going?

AFC AdamLondon: Home, it's a shit night.

HB: We want to get in.

AFC AdamLondon: You can't, it's closing.

HB: Oh man, why are you alone?

AFC AdamLondon: None of those boring airheads interest me.

HB: Really? I'm sure you could take anyone you wanted.

AFC AdamLondon: You really don't understand me at all do you?

HB: I do. (leans in for a hug)

I hold her tight, and we move from the door.

AFC AdamLondon: So what's the plan now?

HB: I've left my keys with my friend at the other club.

We fluff talk while still in each other's arms. She explains she is drunk. I see it as an excuse so she can kiss me.

We kiss. Her friend leaves. I suggest we go back to mine as it's warmer. We do. She stays the night. She escalates.

The end.

AFC AdamLondon

Then London was about to really know who I was.

Shabnam from Big Brother In my bed ... I've said it before, use Social Proof!: June 23, 2007

Hey Guys,

I'm always up for improving my game. My entourage game has become a great asset in doing so. Entourage game has become like my magic silver surfboard.

Anywho, last night I was out on one of our Entourage nights. The social proof runs thick and fast nowadays. There were 35 women, a VIP section, and 4 guys. Also, I've been doing it long enough that not only do the staff know me but almost every other table knows me too. This includes an additional 40 girls.

In essence, I know almost the entire club scene in London. If I don't know them, I know someone that does.

Big Brother Contestant Shabnam gets introduced to me.

Random Important Person: Shabnam, I'd like you to meet Adam. He is one of the big players in the club world and owns a company called ***** which teaches men how to meet and attract women.

Shabnam: I've heard of you

AFC AdamLondon: Really? I didn't know my Dad was here.

Randomer: I'll let you guys talk

Shabnam: Yeah, everyone seems to know you.

AFC AdamLondon: Really? I doubt that. So what's your name?

Shabnam: Don't you know who I am? I've been on TV recently.

AFC AdamLondon: I don't believe in TV, I'm too busy living my life.

Shabnam: I like that. Call me Shags.

AFC AdamLondon: Ok... Tell me three interesting things about yourself.

We fluff talk. I tell her it's too loud and isolate. She is so out of her league she doesn't realise it. She goes to k-close but I pull away.

We move to the bar. The manager nods to me in that *Adam, why don't you order yourself and your girl a drink on the house* kinda way.

I order a drink, the barman brings it and motions that I should pay money. The manager says, "Don't worry about it."

The barman smiles and tells us to have a good night.

AFC AdamLondon: Are you spontaneous?

Shabnam: Yes, the most spontaneous person you'll ever meet.

AFC AdamLondon: Good, lets go to the park

Shabnam: Now?

AFC AdamLondon: Yes.

We go to the park and sit by the river. We are stopped about 100 times on the way. Naturally I assume they are community guys who have recognised me from my field reports. Unbelievably they wanted their photo with her.

Sitting on a bench by the river she strokes my dick through my trousers. With her mouth.

She needs to pee. I suggest my house. We go home. She is now asleep in my bed. I can't really write up too much more as I can hear her waking.

May add more later. What a night.

AFC AdamLondon

At that point I really started breaking down my game. I did a lot of research into Social Proof and why it was so powerful. Finally I was able to really translate my teachings into something concrete.

Social Proof by AFC AdamLondon: June 25, 2007

Hey Guys,

Following on from the recent interest into Social Proof I thought I'd post this up. Most of this I've cut and pasted from my own handouts from the AFC AdamLondon Social Proof Seminars I was doing earlier this year on the subject. I thought I may do a book but everyone seems to be doing that. So I thought why not share it with ya'll. Feel free to cut and paste this and post it all over the internet! I'm more interested in the knowledge getting out than making a few quid.

Social proof is essentially a means to generate pre-selection and propinquity.

Pre-selection was a form of attraction that I feel was adequately outlined in a psychological test covered last year by Benedict Jones. The theory behind pre-selection has been around since the mid 1900's and arguably before, however I feel this test sums it up more than well enough for our purposes.

The Test

Benedict Jones Test 05.02.06

Female participants first viewed eight pairs of male faces and indicated which face in each pair they preferred and how strongly they preferred it. Following this, participants viewed a slideshow where they saw the same pairs of male faces, but in which a woman was shown looking at one of the men with either a happy expression (i.e. smiling) or a relatively negative (i.e. neutral) expression. After the slide show, participants repeated the initial face preference test.

Results

For female participants, a paired samples t-test comparing the change in mean strength of preference for target faces in the happy and neutral conditions showed that the increase in preference for faces that were smiled at by women during the observation phase was greater than that for faces that were looked at by women with neutral expressions.

So we can see from the test that women generally prefer men that other women are already attracted to. As certain emotions can be ambiguous to see from a distance or without understanding the context a harmless smile will often be perceived by others as a signature of attraction.

Therefore the more people you speak to in a room and leave feeling good about themselves with regards to you, the more pre-selection you will generate. This could be done by anything from going around taking pictures of people, to getting everyone to dance, to buying everyone a drink, to just saying hi to everyone you meet.

However Social Proof is even more powerful as it also generates Propinquity, and this is a form of comfort.

Preselection = Attraction

Propinquity = Comfort

Attraction + Comfort = Lay

(Awesome formula, eh? Who said I was crap at math!)

Propinquity is the term used to describe a physical proximity, special bond, or some form of kinship between things. Psychology views this as one of the leading triggers in interpersonal or social attraction. It roughly relates to being close to someone else in some form or another. This could be in physical terms, such as you live in the same area as someone, or not so physical, such as you both belong to the same association. The closer the proximity, the higher the propinquity. For example, those living on the same floor in a building have a higher propinquity than those on different floors.

In this Diagram we can see that A and B would both be attracted to C as C lies within both of A and B's Circle. Likewise C would be attracted to both A and B and would have the option of choosing either. D is the outsider of the group, and therefore holds the lowest levels of attraction to any of the other parties.

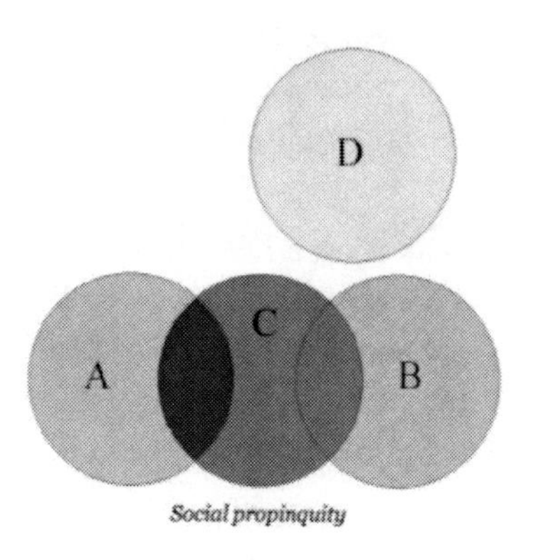

Social propinquity

The propinquity effect is the tendency for people to form friendships or romantic relationships with those whom they encounter often. In other words, relationships tend to be formed between those who have a high propinquity. It was first theorized by psychologists Leon Festinger, Stanley Schachter, Kurt Lewin and Kurt Bach, in what came to be called as, the Westgate studies conducted at MIT University in 1950.

Propinquity can be more than just physical distance. For example, residents of an apartment building living near a stairway tend to have more friends from other floors than others. Propinquity also applies to social groups. These could consist of class mates, friendships, social circles or even work colleagues. This also explains the tendency for teachers to date teachers, members of the police force to date each other and so on.

In 1956 Alan C Kerckhoff conducted a study on residential propinquity. Around 70% of the married couples lived within 20 blocks of their partner before marriage. This seems obvious when you think about it yet it is something people don't really think about.

It seems strange to say that just being close to somebody generates attraction, yet if you notice the amount of IOI's you get if you see a girl every morning on the same train, or from someone who lives in the apartment block opposite you there are a lot. You will almost always begin to say hello every day. Obviously this isn't the be all and end all, however it is the start. Social proof enables us to generate this by regularly creating this initial spark whenever we vibe with a room showing that the room is our social circle and that they are part of it.

It is powerful because it is a passive form of game. When ran correctly it enables you to get opened. My wing and best friend Jim Stark used this to close his incredibly hot current girlfriend who is a slim, blonde, model type and at least 6 inches taller than Jim. She actually asked him, "Who are you? Why does everyone seem to know you?"

The fact that it requires little outer game and instead primarily relies on having fun and possessing a solid inner game frame to work from makes it something that people can get to grips with easily without jeopardising their own personality.

It has been the basis of my game since I started in the community and is, in my mind, the reason I have done as well as I have, so quickly. Though I am always looking to make myself better. I have seen past tutors and wings of mine stare at me as with only social proof and a few simple AFC lines, I have managed to close girls that blew them out previously. Then watched them completely alter their game to focus on Social Proof to amazing effect.

You want the magic pill? It doesn't exist. Social Proof is the next best thing.

AFC AdamLondon

Everything was getting easier. People were interested in flash game, the art of getting incredibly quick results. I developed an almost fool proof way to get a number.

---

10 Second Number Close Routine: June 26, 2007

Hey guys,

I haven't posted any of this stuff for a while as I've been concentrating on social proof and my social circle.

However I developed this after watching *Keys to the VIP*, in my attempt to perform the speediest number close out of my mates as me and my wings had a race to see who could close the fastest.

It's more for laughs than anything else.

Anyway, it could be used for game but really it's just an exercise to show how easy it is to get a strangers number.

It might be good for all newbies to try out as an exercise in Inner Game. It does take a lot of guts, especially if you try to escalate.

PUA: I'm sorry to bother you, but my phone doesn't seem to be getting any signal and I'm waiting for a call. Would you mind giving me a quick call to see if the call goes through?

HB: Sure. (Give number, she dials)

Close. It's that easy.

2nd stage, possibly through text message a bit later

PUA: Mwahahaha, now I have your phone number! You've been picked up. Only joking, I'm not really a weird stalker...

Enjoy it, it's a game.

AFC AdamLondon

---

1 Year of Game! AFC AdamLondon: June 29, 2007, 12:28:43 PM

Well, what can I say? What a ride.

I've written a few posts about my past already so that I can cut to the juicy stuff in this post.

My first ever approach was on a bootcamp of Catnaps where we played Kissing Bandit. I was the first to do it and knew that if I was going to get good I'd have to apply myself fully. What he said, I did.

I was lucky enough to do pretty well on my first bootcamp. I even managed to close a hot blonde that a whole bunch of other students had been blown out from. Looking back I realise I did it by not showing need and DHVing. At the time I thought it was luck.

I went out with Humjob and did a bit of daygame. I was blown out by some girls that I wouldn't even bother to open were I to meet them today

I was introduced to James DeMarco, Sky and Tomcat. I managed to offer free PR for the School of Seduction in return for PU lessons. That's when things really stepped up. I got to meet all the instructors they brought on from their bootcamps like Beckster, Bullboy, Lord Mega, Raven, Jim Stark, and others.

There were issues with some of the founders and instructors, but since then I've learnt that is kinda how things go in the community. On the whole however, the experience was unbelievable.

I created a few tips and tricks of my own.

Probably the most prolific to my game was the limbo routine. Whip out your belt and play limbo in the club. Little did I know that this little game would become Project Entourage.

I had got Flash Game down pretty well and had managed a few five minute and three minute k-closes.

Then I went into overdrive. I went out every single night. Seven days a week, every week for at least two hours to Leicester Square.

AMOG Scott, my flat mate, told me it was a waste of time, and that I was even more geeky than him. That was saying something as he was sitting indoors painting toy soldiers. Still, I practised and practised.

Then after about a month I went to a club with AMOG Scott. He told me he'd show me how it should be done. He approached a really hot chick caveman style, but did it in front of her friends. He wasn't completely congruent with it and she blew him out. I approached smiling, did a quick dance move and then raised my hand in a "whatever" kind of way and walked back to Scott only to have her follow me across the club and spin me around to dance with her.

AMOG Scott was shocked. He wanted to learn. Two days later he was out with us. Me, Tomcat and AMOG Scott went out with a video camera. We played the marriage opener. Never have I since had so much fun whilst sarging as those days. They were hysterical. I'm sure it wasn't proper game. Hell, I'm sure it wasn't congruent with my personality, but it was fun. One night we got like 30 number closes between us all written on the same paper. It got to the point that the girls were highlighting their numbers to make sure we called them in preference. Preselection was beginning to become internalised in my head. I even managed to get a one minute k-close on film.

I secured a whole bunch of coverage for the School of Seduction and even got a piece in FHM. People started to say I was good at game so I changed my name to AFC AdamLondon. This way people would realise I wasn't that great and I had loads to learn.

I started sarging regularly in night clubs. I had made some contacts through the School and a few friends in the clubs.

That's when I went to Umbaba. I saw a table of models and knew I had to open them. I spent the whole night trying it, getting blown out, retrying and retrying. Eventually I just asked one of them if they could teach me what I would need to know in order to learn how to get girls as beautiful as them. It worked. They introduced me to each other, and took me under their wing for the night. As more models joined the party I was treated as one of their own.

I realised that the new girls arriving assumed I was "in" and so they treated me incredibly warmly. I got a close. I knew that the trick to getting the hot ones was to be introduced to them. I met the Princesses, a group of hot party girls who knew everyone in London. A few friendly chats later and bingo... I was an honorary princess.

I got a wing, my first regular one since joining the community, Jim Stark. I love this guy more than you could know. We went out constantly. Every night. We opened everything. We learnt I had a new drive. I wanted to be fast.

I was bored of standard conversation and routines. I wanted to merge the lines. I opened with qualifications and moved to close fast. I was getting results. In fact, whether he'll admit it or not, he was shocked.

My standard routine/conversation stack was now something like this:

"Hey everyone in here seems pretty boring. In fact, I was just saying to my friend that I bet no one has anything interesting to say about themselves. Tell me three interesting things about yourself."

I would *um* and *ah* over the first answer and compliment the other two.

The input into their life would give me a lot to talk about though I'd often just say, "You know what, you are quite interesting. We go out to parties all the time, do you have any cool friends you could bring? Cool, you should come along. What's the best way to get in contact with you?"

Times moved faster and TomCat approached me with his new business idea on PU. I decided to work with him on one condition; that we didn't make it community oriented. I loved the forum so much and had gained so much from it, I didn't want to view it as a commercial venture. Rather, I would teach myself directly to it and we would find customers elsewhere. He agreed. I wouldn't charge for my forum services if I thought I could feasibly pull it off. The fact is I didn't. I'd become flakey and cancel on people to see the girls.

OMG the girls.

I have over 200 phone numbers in my phone right now from girls I have sarged in the last three months (since getting my new phone) alone. I've cut down on my sarging a lot from last year.

At one point I was having sex four times a day with a different girl. I had so much I couldn't get it up anymore and had to cut down.

Models, actresses, goths, Americans, two girls at once... I was traveling to countries to meet girls for the first time having escalated over the phone to the point I could f-close on arrival. I could see attraction in their eyes. I could see IOI's everywhere.

So many beautiful women, each more beautiful than the last.

Yet I always wanted to learn more. I wanted to understand it all, I still do.

I have been blown out countless times yet in the last six months I have been blown off a lot more. I have been slapped, beaten and sworn at, yet I have been kissed, loved and adored. I used to believe no one would find me attractive, yet now I assume attraction with every girl I meet.

I have met some of my greatest friends and business partners due to this forum.

I created my alter-ego, AFC AdamLondon. *Women want me, Men want to be me.*

I slept with someone who was star struck when she recognised me from *The London Paper.*

I am currently dating an incredibly beautiful cheerleader from Texas.

Despite all this, my greatest triumphs have been the guys on this forum whom I have helped improve their lives.

It's been one hell of a year. I love all of you. Do you know how many of you have told me to change my name from AFC to PUA? In fairness, I've lost count.

Well he is just my alter ego. He is a frame I enter when I want to get into state.

The fact is, I'll always be AFC. I like it that way. I'm a sad little geek always more content to play with Dungeons and Dragons and rubber swords than go out to clubs and meet women.

Now, thanks to this community, I am comfortable saying I'm good with women. Though I'm still not there yet. It's a long road, and as someone wrote in here recently, another little gem gleaned from this community to be added to my life, the journey is the destination.

I sign off my posts as AFC AdamLondon except for this one.

Thank you guys. I love you all

Adam

....

One of my best friends followed that with this.

I have now known Adam for a year and it has been a very intense time. We have laughed, argued and had many good times together.

Adam is one of the most loyal people I know he would stand by me and his friends in good and bad. He even lost his job for it and turned down better offers from other companies so he could stay and teach with his friend.

The reason Adam learnt so fast and just "got it" is because he is honest with himself and admits his mistakes. He is not afraid of making mistakes in front of anyone, not even his girlfriends.

Of all the game theory this is one of the most important aspects that makes Adam great at game.

I know many people that are good and they tend to only think about themselves when they are in the field. Adam always makes sure you are doing OK and if you need any help because he cares. I remember he once said, "There is only one thing that gives real joy in life and that is to help other people"

Adam is always busy and when I ask him why his answer is, "Because I got to take this guy out and help him." I would ask if he is getting paid and he would say "Nooo, it is not about the money."

Sometimes in life we come across people that don't care that much about money and really want to help people even when they know they will never get anything back from that person. Adam is one of those people.

I know Adam loves me and I think it is because I am ginger, but it could also be because I took him to the doctor when his dick was falling off. Who knows?

The fact is the world needs more people like Adam, people that want to help others. So the next time you want to post and start an argument with someone on the forum, think about the fact that you could have spent your time helping someone else out there who really needed it.

Life is short and your energy is limited so use it for something useful.

Learn to love the world and focus more on helping others and you will focus less on your self. The EGO comes from selfishness and I promise you that the best cure for the fear of rejection is to love the world around you and focus on other peoples needs, not your own.

That is your answer to why Adam is good at game.

Love, Tom

I now understood social proof to a level where it could be generated cold, without even bringing a mass amount of people to a club.

FR - Social Proof from Cold: July 06, 2007

Heya Guys,

As you are all well aware by now, I firmly believe in the power of social proof. However I haven't been able to write much new stuff on it as unfortunately my proof has become so large that I know every major club in central London. Now there isn't really such a thing as a cold set.

When I got invited to Kensington to see a club I hadn't been to before I jumped at the chance to exercise the old sargin' muscles.

Naturally I took the tools of the game with me: my wing and a pair of girls. Why go with anything less? You need the girls for entry and need the wing to game. This should be your aim as standard practice for club game.

Amika

Set 1

So we hit the club and split up, I head straight to the promo girls. I vaguely recognise one that worked at Cafe De Paris from back when I was in the SoS.

AFC AdamLondon: Hey I know you. Didn't you used to work at Cafe De Paris? (social proof)

HB: Yeah I did, I think I remember...

AFC AdamLondon: I doubt it, you had thousands of customers... (Change focus to other promo girls)

AFC AdamLondon: Isn't it difficult to breathe in that corset? That can't be fun to wear.

Other Promo HB: Yeah it is kinda tight, not fun at all, especially when it keeps twisting around.

AFC AdamLondon: Rather you than me. Have fun tonight, try not to work to hard. Oh these are my friends (quick introduction to wing and girls). See you guys around.

Eject.

Take wing to bar, leave girls to get chatted up by random guys. We order a drink and are mildly surprised by the fact that it's all free. Head over to a two set of guys.

AFC AdamLondon: Hey guys, what's the occasion here?

Guy: Free Drinks!

AFC AdamLondon: Awesome! Actually I noticed that. But what's the reason for the free drinks?

Guy: Wu-Tang Clan private party.

AFC AdamLondon: Oh yeah, I heard that may be going on. Cool, who you guys with?

Guy: Actually I'm the accountant for the club.

More boring fluff talk. Eject.

Random good looking, clean shaven, well built guy

The club is beginning to fill up. We watch the girls get chatted up by random guys. I note the issues with the guys. They are showing too much direct interest, over using Kino, intentions are too clear and there is too much proximity.

I like one of the girls, so figure I'd better ensure I don't lose out.

AFC AdamLondon: Hey cutie, you scored!

HB: No, he's not really my type.

AFC AdamLondon: But he really liked you, like I think he really wanted you. You can tell right?

HB: Yeah, but he's too full on and sleazy.

AFC AdamLondon: What's wrong with sleazy? Doesn't that work?

HB: Eww No.

AFC AdamLondon: (Grins to himself)

AMOGing complete, time to move on.

One of our HB's spots a cute promo girl.

HB: Wow, she is cute. I have a girl crush on her.

AFC AdamLondon (Noted)

I sit and chat to my wing for a bit, mostly so I don't look like a chode, and also to discuss good sets and eat the teryaki beef that is being handed around.

Cute Girl crush promo girl approaches.

Promo girl: You having a good night?

AFC AdamLondon: Lets see... free food, free drink, good music, um yes. You?

Promo Girl: Yes of course.

AFC AdamLondon: Even though you can't breathe in that corset?

Promo Girl: Hahah, OMG, yes it's so bad.

AFC AdamLondon: Awesome, oh wait, where's that accent from?

Promo girl: South Wales.

AFC AdamLondon: Like Newport?

Promo Girl: 25 minutes from there.

AFC AdamLondon: Why London? Or was it to pursue a career as a corset wearing promo girl?

Promo Girl: Yep, that's it.

AFC AdamLondon: I knew it.

Promo Girl: No it's to become an actress.

AFC AdamLondon: Oh I actually know a few actors. They're always "in between jobs." Still, it's a good industry. All about networking, right?

Promo Girl: Yes.

AFC AdamLondon: Well let's meet up sometime outside of this worky venue stuff, on equal grounds and see if we can share contacts.

Promo Girl: Ok.

Close.

Then I introduce her to our HB's. Once she leaves one of the HB's suddenly speaks.

HB: Girl crush over... pretty package, shame the box is empty.

Entourage!

I look to my wing.

AFC AdamLondon: Lets make our own Entourage. From

scratch, for fun!

I jump on a couch and start dancing. None of that fancy hopping stuff, just one fist thrown into the air! It's a good dance move for those that can't hop.

As I'm dancing I look for the best girls in the club. It's not the best night for pickings actually, but still manage to find a nice two set dancing hard. I point at them and call them up next to me. (Leading and compliance)

They get dancing and then I see another girl partying and drag her up.

I build a quick bit of kino escalation and the next thing you know the girls are all over me literally rubbing their bodies up against me, running their fingers through my hair over my bum, etc. It's like an Entourage night, only built from scratch at the club.

I only got one photo of it from my wing but it kinda gives an idea as to what was happening. Everyone was watching and from that point on, all sets were completely warm to us and opening us.

We took the girls numbers and invited them along for a future party. The social proof trap will ensure a close, if I or one of our guys want it.

As I said, it's rare for me to actually be in a situation where I can get to do this. From a personal game point of view I found it incredibly valuable as I got to see that the Entourage game I set up wasn't a fluke and is definitely reproducible, not only by my students but also by me as well.

Good fun night, exactly how it should be.

AFC AdamLondon

Social Proof Cheat - It's indirect... if you don't like indirect look away now! July 15, 2007

Ok so how do you pull the really hot girls using social proof?

Let's imagine a situation where it is only you and a wing out sarging. Eeep, AFC AdamLondon's worst nightmare. No girls! Arghghghghg!

Ok wait, I'm over it.

The fact is you have to start somewhere. I recently wrote a post about social proofing from cold in the FR section. However it doesn't break down many of the actual tactics fully.

So here I'm going to write up a brief example of something you can do to help you social proof from cold.

Enter the club with your wing; open everyone casually. By this I mean ask where toilets are, smile and tell them to have a great night, casually open people at the bar with, "Wow, service is pretty slow here tonight, eh?"

This is all standard conversation accompanied with a smile and a "Have a good night." The idea is that very quickly people will be friendlier towards you and you aren't the random weird looking guy hitting on everyone. Instead you are just a friendly guy who happens to speak to everyone around them. You are a socially comfortable guy.

Then you open a set. Make sure that as quickly as possible, you ask them a question that will involve them giving you a detailed answer.

Something like;

"What are the three best places in the world to visit or that you'd like to visit, and why?"

Then lock yourself into a casual position where it would appear that they are hitting on you. Leaning against a wall or seated in a chair. As they lean into you to give their answers, you can look around the room giving IOI's.

This will give the impression of a hot chick chatting YOU up to others around you. It's a much better position to be in than having people think you are chatting them up. Then you should be able to trade serious IOI's with someone across the room, of an equal hotness to the "tool" you are using to convey preselection.

You may not pull your current set but you will pull the girl you are trading IOI's with.

To increase your chances even further close the new hot girl completely indirectly. Tell her you're organising a pub crawl or giant water fight and inviting as many people as possible and that she should invite people as well. Whatever.

When she turns up and see a whole bunch of other hot chicks all over you preselection and attraction kicks in.

I hope that helps.

As usual, if there are any questions just ask away.

AFC AdamLondon

Though no amount of game can protect you from some girls...

Messed Up - report: Woman are lovely creatures aren't they? July 28, 2007

Guys,

Last night I spot this cute little party chick who always attends the same parties we do. She looks a little worse for wear so I figure I'll check her out.

AFC AdamLondon: Hey cutie, how's tricks?

HB: Hey baby. Look after me, I don't know where I've been

AFC AdamLondon: Ok babe, you're in good hands now. Lets get you into the bar area so you can sit

HB: OK... you know you're cute right?

AFC AdamLondon: I'm really not that great when you aren't drunk.

HB: ...

AFC AdamLondon:...

Then she leans in to kiss me.

AFC AdamLondon: (Whilst pulling away) Sorry babe, I don't kiss drunk girls

HB: .. Oh go on...I like you

AFC AdamLondon: I have a girlfriend and am intending to stay as faithful as I can.

She moves in for the kiss again. This time as I pull away she says..

HB: I don't feel well.

And then she vomits... all over my shirt and trousers.

If I had kissed her that would have been my mouth instead of my shirt.

Women... Beautiful creations.

AFC AdamLondon

Re: Wise words from AMOG Scott: August 03, 2007

So last night AMOG Scott was out again. He hasn't been out for a long time.

He spots a student sitting by the bar watching a PUA in set.

AMOG Scott: You know, you won't get a girl by watching her or talking about game. You get her by speaking to her.

Student: But what do I say?

AMOG Scott: *Hello* has always worked for me.

Student: OK..

He approaches... he ends up salsa dancing with her...

Wise words from AMOG Scott.

Positivity: August 03, 2007

I'm a positive person. Sickeningly so. I know it. People around me know it. It's who I am and I can't change it. I've been like it my whole life.

I live in my own little reality where I only see the good in people and always wish them well. If I get shit on or hurt I forgive them and try to fix things. If I can't then I simply move them out of my life.

Ironically many people refuse to believe this is true, they look for the first sign that I waver from being positive and helpful. On numerous occasions in my past I've had people jump on a mistake I've made and use it as an excuse to hate me forever. Even those I can't blame because I understand why they would come to that conclusion.

Will positivity work for you? Only if you want it to.

There's an old Psychologist joke about how many psychologists it takes to change a lightbulb. Only one, but the bulb has to want to make the change.

There will always be fads in PU and, in fact, in everything. When one idea seems better than another a heap of people flock to it in the hope that it will make them better and give them access to their wildest dreams.

There will always be people pioneering these movements and capitalising on the new-found fame and love they have obtained. That is life. If you want something to work for you, it will. It will work to the best of your capabilities.

You do have limits but you will only know what they are when you reach for them and then push them further.

Push them as far as you can comfortably go. That's how you become the best you can be.

Today at the gym I added 5 more pull ups to my standard set ... I did it to prove to myself that I could. No other reason.

Was my limit the old one or the new one? I'll tell you something; my limit is a lot further away than either. I'm just not ready for it...Yet.

I'll continue being the best I can be as it's all I can be. Be the same. If you want to be positive, do it. Not because I told you to, or anyone else did. Do it because it is something you want to try. If you don't, then don't.

The beauty of life is that we have one universal freedom, the freedom of choice.

Use that freedom

Choose.

AFC AdamLondon

....

Around this time I met a girl... one who would cause me more trouble than I could possibly imagine. It started like this:

....

AFC AdamLondon vs Justin Timberlake: July 09, 2007, 10:17:20 PM

The ultimate AMOG showdown!

So here I am sitting at home on the forum. I would like you all to know how great I am feeling right now. My stomach is full of quite possibly one of my favourite meals of all time.

I simmered some garlic and butter with some cajun spices and then added some king prawns. I bust out a few broccoli, asparagus and carrots, steamed and lightly buttered. Then cooked some tomato and basil rice and mixed in some fresh tomato puree so that I could set it in a small cup and turn it upside down on the plate. Added a few sunblushed tomatoes and garnish, and voila! It was a great meal.

There is one plate left if anyone wants it. That's the one my hot date for this evening was supposed to be eating.

So she was en route to me from the local train station that's 2 minutes away. I start serving food. I can almost see it in slow motion: she crosses the road en route to me and who turns up?

Justin Fucking Timberlake. Ha.

She stops. She can't breath and begins to cry. Dude, this is serious. I found out all of this from her a few minutes after when she called to cancel the meal.

She ran upstairs to her hotel room, got changed, and is now on her way to the restaurant to flirt with him.

Some normal girl may have no chance, however this is an incredibly hot US chick who has done this countless of times before with other celebrities and has closed. She has been waiting to meet Justin Timberlake for nine years.

Anywho, I did what any self respecting PUA should do. I sat

down to eat my meal whilst watching *Ghost Rider*, which I hadn't seen and I know she wouldn't want to watch it so figured I'd get it in now. Then I sent her a text detailing exactly how to social proof the venue and change from bar to bar to get an introduction and escalate to help her close him (she knows I do game).

Am I upset? The verdict is still out.

However I have had a good meal and get to finish watching the movie. At the end of the night I may get to say that me and Justin Timberlake went head to head for a girl (whether he knew it or not) and yet that night she lay in my bed.

Man I love this game.

AFC AdamLondon

A lot of people commented to that thread so a short while later I put up my response.

Re: AFC AdamLondon Vs Justin Timberlake: July 10, 2007, 06:28:26 PM

Hey guys, cheers for the responses.

It was definitely JT, I saw the photos last night when they came back to my place.

Skeletor, you are 100% right, she definitely would have slept with him. The fact is, as we mentioned, the frame was completely wrong for her to close him and I was comfortable with that. I'm sure a lot of girls would do it if given the chance, purely for the fame factor. However it would just be an ONS, and does that bother me? I don't know. If it had happened I would have to think about how I felt about it, however the odds were squarely in my favour.

She felt bad for standing me up so she took me out all day and is taking me to dinner tonight. She has been attentive all day.

I wound her up by telling her if I had gone for a celebrity I would have closed and that her game sucks.

I have to admit, I really like her. She has game, is none needy, incredibly hot and has a gorgeous US accent to die for. I have no idea if she is interested in a relationship with me and after hinting at it I have decided to leave it to the fates. She is heading back to the US so I doubt we could handle the long distance of it.

It's not like I couldn't pull someone just as hot, it's more that I wouldn't find someone else that would want me to give them an aeroplane at 2 a.m.

Don't ask.

AFC AdamLondon

Despite the US girl, I was still going out partying. I was keeping myself occupied and trying not to fall into that same oneitis head space that had lured me into messing up a few months earlier.

In so many ways I was a completely different person to how I was a year earlier. Situations I found myself in were dealt with in a completely different way. I no longer got upset as easily. I had learnt the ability to remain unreactive.

FR AMOG (alpha male of the group) vs AFC AdamLondon: August 04, 2007

Hey guys,

So last night I was out with my Entourage and I figured I would share a story with you from the night.

It's vaguely related to something that happened about eight months ago when I first started sarging with Sheriff regularly. I pride myself on being pretty unreactive, however on this specific occasion something got to me.

We were walking into Chinawhites and were building up social proof by chatting to some random guys in the queue when suddenly a girl walked by that I knew. The guy next to me starts speaking,

Queue Guy: See, that girl that is exactly the kind of girl that would fuck anyone for money.

AFC AdamLondon: What?

Queue Guy: You can see she just spreads her legs open for any guy with a bit of cash.

AFC AdamLondon: Actually mate, you're wrong. That girl is nothing like that at all

Queue Guy: Yes she is, you can see cash slut written all over her face.

AFC AdamLondon: Look here you prick, not every girl goes for cash. Some people actually have depth.

When have you ever heard me like that before? I can tell you it's pretty rare. So Sheriff comments.

Sherrif: Why did you react?

AFC AdamLondon: Because he was a dick

Sherrif: Nah, you reacted because he struck a nerve... he said something you didn't like.

AFC AdamLondon: What do you mean?

Sherrif: You didn't like the fact that it's possible that a girl would like someone purely for money because you aren't rich.

He was right. I've grown up from a very poor background and actually don't have much disposable income. The guy hit a nerve and I let him get to me.

So I made a conscious decision to try to not let it affect me in the future. To be fair, I think I've done pretty good.

Then last night I got to test myself.

I was dancing around our tables and I have to admit Entourage was really kicking last night. We had over 60 girls on the list and 40 in the VIP area. Most were dancers, so it was really smashing. Four girls were getting hit on by this sleazy, slightly tipsy Indian guy.

He was grabbing their hands and essentially giving them hassle. I spot one girl and mouth the words, "Are you guys OK?"

She shakes her head so I move in.

AFC AdamLondon: Heya duddy, how you doing?

AMOG: I'm good, thanks.

AFC AdamLondon: I'm sorry to have to tell you this mate but this is a private table. The girls need a little more space.

AMOG: I'm just dancing with them.

AFC AdamLondon: I know buddy, but it's one of their birthday's and they just want to dance together. Would you mind giving them a little bit of space?

AMOG: Yeah, it's cool, I'm not dancing with them. Dance with me!

AFC AdamLondon: Nah, mate. Have a good night.

So I move off, but stay near the girls just in case.

He starts staring at them and I mean literally staring. One of the girls stops dancing and stares back. I take the hint and move back on the guy.

AFC AdamLondon: Hey buddy, you're really going to have to move away, the girls are feeling hassled.

AMOG: I'm not hassling anyone.

AFC AdamLondon: You're hassling the girls; they don't want you staring at them or dancing with them. Seriously buddy you're gonna have to move away.

AMOG: They want to dance with me.

AFC AdamLondon: (Turns to girls) Do you guys want to dance with this guy?

HB's: Yes

AFC AdamLondon: What?!?!

AMOG: *smug grin* See!

Now the problem is, the club is loud and hot women aren't always so quick to catch onto things. Thankfully they elaborate.

HB's: Yes, we want him to go.

AFC AdamLondon: So DO YOU WANT TO DANCE WITH HIM?

HB's: Ohh, no of course not!

AMOG: ...

AFC AdamLondon: Sorry buddy, have a good night and I'll see you around.

AMOG: Talk to me; let me tell you something. I'm kind of a big deal.

AFC AdamLondon: Cool.

AMOG: I mean, I don't want to brag but I earn a lot of money.

AFC AdamLondon: Awesome.

AMOG: Women like me because I have a lot of money, they like it when I buy them drinks.

AFC AdamLondon: That's great.

AMOG: What I mean is, your girls want my drinks.

AFC AdamLondon: So far tonight I've given them a bottle of

Cristal, two rounds of shots and two bottles of vodka. I think they've probably drunk too much. Either way, they really don't need you to buy them drinks.

AMOG: Look, I make a lot of money, ok? More than you.

AFC AdamLondon: That's probably true, still I'm happy.

AMOG: Look I can tell you have a boring and tedious job.

AFC AdamLondon: Cool.

AMOG: Like what is it?

AFC AdamLondon: Look mate we don't need to do this, have a great night. I'm off.

AMOG: No! Tell me what do you do? I know it's boring and tedious

AFC AdamLondon: You really wanna do this?

AMOG: Yes! Tell me!

AFC AdamLondon: I teach guys how to pick up women.

AMOG: Don't lie. Tell me the truth.

AFC AdamLondon: I teach guys how to pick up women, ask anyone at my table.

AMOG: (turns to Sheriff) What does he do for a living?

Sherrif: He teaches guys how to pick up women. You don't believe him? There are 40 women at this table and only 3 men. You think that's a coincidence?

AMOG: Look, my money makes me happy.

AFC AdamLondon: OK then, lets do it like this. You take your money and go and be happy on your table, I'll take my girls and be happy on mine. Have a great night!

Off he went.

I still reacted a bit and kinda wish I hadn't. Still, I'm far from perfect. Though internally he really didn't get to me in a bad way. I didn't have that terrible feeling I had before or the anger. Just the usual calm sense of self I normally have in those situations. So a small personal triumph!

AFC AdamLondon

The truth about game - It's a fine line: August 08, 2007,

Hey guys,

I'm battling with the hardest set of my life at the moment and dealing with an AMOG so powerful it never relents.

The set is my new girlfriend and the AMOG is me.

I met a girl as some of you know. I like her, I like her a lot. In fact I like her to the point that I've stopped f-closing other girls.

She is everything I have ever dreamed a wife would be yet unfortunately she is three years away from a point where she would consider getting married. I understand this, I know it, it's a fact. Details surround this that I can't put here, but that's how it is.

The problem is the truth in game.

Game can be used as a shield. It's something to hide behind to avoid actually facing up to life. Some of the best PUA's in the world are, for lack of better words, ageing, single, men still lusting after young girls. Myself included.

I got into the game to learn how to get girls, but what then? The fact is we aren't often prepared for success as we don't believe the techniques work as well as they do. However they do work.

The new temptation is to get better and better girls. At some point as humans we should ask ourselves when it stops? When do we just settle down?

I did and I met a girl. I want to settle down with her and here is where the real issues kick in.

I can't stop gaming. It is horrible. Every interaction is full of negs, qualifications and kino. The girls are still attracted yet I only want my girl, in as AFC a way as you can get.

Though this is only one side of the tightrope. You see, on the other side I have the fact that I want to be AFC with my girl.

I want to believe she likes me for who I truly am and that I can tell her how much I want her and that we will be together forever. Though this will invariably push her away.

Yet if she saw the women on the other side fighting for me and me gaming them, she would run just as fast.

So I walk the line between the two, giving comfort, fighting off the girls, being AFC yet allowing space and demonstrating stories. I realise that putting the entire equation together is the hardest set I will ever do. Would it be this difficult if I didn't know game? I don't know. I definitely wouldn't understand what was going on, however I wouldn't have to worry about my own dark temptation.

It's easily controlled, though what scares me is if she picks up on me being AFC and loses interest. You see, she doesn't have to actually lose interest. I only need my head to believe that she now sees me as an AFC. How do I prove her wrong? Do I accept the temptation on the other side? Fuck 10 other women?

Well, no. That would truly be the killing blow.

It's a fine line.

"Grief is the price we pay for love" - 911 memorial in London.

AFC AdamLondon

That was another one that received a lot of comments. I posted my reply.

Re: The truth about game - It's a fine line: August 10, 2007

Hey guys!

Thank you all so much! It means a lot to get the support of you all.

The fact is, I kind of have to get on with this one alone. As the guys have said, I do need a deeper purpose and I'm working towards it. I had to face up to the fact that I want this to be serious so I don't screw it up. There's been a few other cool girls who I've pushed away by continuing to game. I'm not giving up yet though. I've got a few big things in the pipeline and a lot more to learn, though I'm not k-closing or f-closing for the time being.

Personally I think I'm walking the line well, and the thought of other girls really doesn't interest me right now. The only fear is the temptation, though I seem pretty able to hold it off for now.

I'll keep you guys posted. There will either be a big ass wedding or I'll hit the game like you've never seen an AFC hit the game before!

AFC AdamLondon

The girl in the US was not really telling me what she wanted. She had a great ability to keep quiet and refused point blank to confirm if we were dating or not. Still, despite the relationship I was kind of having – or not having – I tried to keep my practice up. So I invented new ways to continue practising.

Day 2 - The Interview: August 17, 2007

So once again I've been thinking of new ways to play with the game.

I've been fiddling with a bit of a model and have been trialing it.

Now at the moment I'm only seeing this one girl as she is special to me. However, that doesn't mean I'm not testing things out and last week I trialed a new technique for setting up a day 2.

Essentially it's a massive form of qualification, which is used to really generate a lot of attraction and get the girl into the frame of trying to get you. Attraction is almost assumed once she jumps through the hoop.

I tested it last week and it's golden.

So I'm in set on the dancefloor,

AFC AdamLondon: Ahh, it would never work between us. You're too short for me.

HB: I'm not short.

AFC AdamLondon: (Compares height) You're shorter than me.

HB: So? I prefer it when men are taller.

AFC AdamLondon: Still, I've only met you in a night club. I'm not sure you're the kinda girl who I'd like outside it. I mean, yes you are hot, but... Look around you there's a lot of hot girls. I need to see what you're like outside. What're you doing this weekend?

HB: Uhh, nothing.

AFC AdamLondon: Ok let's meet up during the day and I can see if I like you outside of the club.

HB: Ok that sounds great!

Now although I used height, I've had great results with age and it would probably work with a whole bunch of other attributes as well. By assuming the attraction, and qualifying you build up a very very strong frame.

Try it out; let me know how it goes!

AFC AdamLondon

Then I cracked something big. I had always realised I played game in a bigger way by not just thinking about the target but everyone else relating to it. I don't know whether it was a lack of sex, a new passion instilled in me because of the US girl, or just a final brainwave. But...

The Metagame: August 18, 2007

For those of you who have been in the game for a while now, you will probably have developed your own style of play. Whether you are following one of the more mainstream methods or have developed your own sense of game, you typically have a sense of sameness to our approach.

For example, some PUAs favour a more direct style. Others prefer to use some form of dance game, whereas others may still use routines, or cocky funny type spur of the moment lines. Whatever your style, there is one thing that does apply to many PUAs, especially those in areas populated with a strong community. Sometimes you can't avoid sarging in the same venue as other PUA's.

You may have a different style to the other PUAs in the area, but the fact is you are competing with other PUAs. Now I understand that some people are fortunate enough to be in areas where there are few PUAs so this wouldn't really apply to them. However, having said this, almost every area will still have naturals, which can sometimes be as bad as their professional PUA counterparts.

The *Metagame* is something that was first used in mathematics as a descriptor for set interaction that governs subset interaction in certain cases. The term was then taken and passed through military and political actions to describe operations or events that were outside the bounds of a normal situation. I suppose it could be described in layman's terms as *thinking outside the box*. It's applications are much more specific than that.

A good example of Metagaming could be one found in politics where a law was passed to placate a specific media sensation. The actual effect of that law however, may be used to further another cause. In this situation "the game" would be the passing of the law, but the Metagame would be the bigger picture into which the passing of the law fits. For example, it could be like using the terrorist act to enable police greater powers to invade privacy. It's an extreme example, but it makes the point)

The idea is that you are playing to the bigger picture. You have a clearly defined set of goals and will tailor your gameplay to achieving that aim, typically by refining your standard set of decisions by using additional information in order to achieve your goal.

For simpler game a related example we can use chess. In chess there is a special set of four moves that can ensure you win the game. If you notice your opponent has used these same four moves in his last six matches in order to win, you could use this additional information in order to secure the victory by assuming he would continue to use them and playing in such a way that they would not work.

So, how does this all relate to game? Well, the fact is, there are some PUAs that flourish in an environment rich with other PUAs and naturals and those that see those venues as something to be avoided. Naturally everyone would prefer to work in a venue full of nothing but hot babes but sometimes you just have to battle it out. This is where it's time to use the Metagame.

You will not always be fortunate enough to have opened the hottest girl in the room first, which means that typically she will have been approached by a number of guys before you. If there are a number of PUAs in the venue, or even some pretty decent naturals, what will set **you** apart from them? If three other guys have used the *jealous girlfriend* opinion opener or made some form of C+F remark about something she is doing or wearing, how will you be able to ensure you stand out?

It's time to fight dirty. Remember, the Metagame is not a friendly way of playing. It involves using all necessary information in order to achieve the goal of getting the girl you want. Do **not** use this on wings, friends or anyone else you care about.

Generally it should be bro's before ho's and that is something to consider carefully before using any of the techniques described below. You have been warned.

The Metagame is big, really big. There is no way I could mention every single possible eventuality as each style of Metagame will have a Metagame to counter it for an infinite number of eventualities. What you are looking to achieve is a mindset where you will be able to calibrate your game to take into account the wider game being played in the room.

You aren't looking at a set as a group of HB's, you are looking at the room and seeking the best plan of attack based on as much of the room as possible. Let's look at this from a social proof point of view. My personal favourite:

Imagine a 2 set of SHB's (super hot babes) being opened by absolutely every guy in the room. The guys are either naturals who just go in sharking or PUAs obeying the 3-second rule. They approach, hit a bitch shield and get blown out (I'll cover what happens if they don't get blown out later). Opinion openers have already been used and the girls "just want to be left alone." How can we break in?

Well we take a look at the bigger picture. This is a simple form of Metagame that most of the community are well aware of. By simply opening a set to the side of the group we wish to approach we can then bounce from that group into the 2 set. By not going completely direct it doesn't appear to be a pickup but rather a very normal form of conversation.

example:

You open a mixed set next to the HB's and get talking to them. Vibe with the group, showing the room that you are adding value to the group. Pretty soon into the conversation you can go around and introduce yourself to everyone in the group and then literally continue introducing yourself into the 2 set. There'll be a moment of awkwardness as they explain they aren't part of the same group, which you can then laugh at with them and then continue introducing yourself to them anyway.

Nothing particularly new there and obviously there are a million other ways to bridge sets but the point is you looked at the room as a means of opening the set rather than working out which opener would work best.

This is the Metagame at it's simplest form. It is a way of dealing with average PUAs and naturals. But what happens if the PUA didn't get blown out of the set?

What if the natural was doing well?

Then we have to AMOG right? Go in and be friendly to the guy? Then we are looking at a situation where it is possibly PUA vs PUA, a true test of who has the best game. However, that may not be a completely fair fight. What if they do have more skill than you or more routines? Maybe they can perform real magic and card tricks. What then?

We need another way of playing something that will knock them down before they have even started. Let's look at how the Metagame would deal with this. We understand from the community that the core principles that govern attraction are

Comfort
Attraction
Seduction

Managing these is a key part of securing the girl. What if we messed with the other PUAs game by altering one of these without them knowing?

Let's take the above example of the 2 HB's and assume that the Natural/PUA didn't get blown out.

As before we could build up social proof by opening the same mixed set then lean over to the 2 HB's and casually remark say, "Hey looks like you've pulled there."

I have used this countless times and will almost always receive the same response.

HB: "I'm sorry, what?"

Then all you do is simply explain what you said.

"The dude there. It looks like you've tagged yourself a new boyfriend"

Now what you have done is completely mess with his game by making him appear completely available. Essentially you have made him gain so much comfort with her, ideally at a point so early into the interaction that she will see the pick up for what it is, and then either blow him out or store him in her pocket and continue looking for better options in the room.

Either way you've just opened the HB in a very warm way and can begin trading knowing glances or "girl signals" with her as she continues to get picked up. Which will make her incredibly receptive to your future advances.

Remember, there is a chance you may miscalibrate. The Metagame isn't 100% perfect as no form of game is. If it turns out that the guy is actually her brother then you could come out looking slightly worse. In which case all you will have to do is re-frame the situation.

The fact is these occurrences are few and far between and hardly warrant avoiding the chance to use solid Metagame.

As you can see all we are doing is using the knowledge we have of the game to affect the other guys chances by miscalibrating him.

This could also be done by altering any of the other factors in his game. For example, if a guy was trying to isolate a girl and close, you could ruin his chances by destroying the mood and joining the two of them. However that wouldn't necessarily paint you in the best light and may appear like you were trying too hard. You wouldn't be using the knowledge, you would be AMOGing.

However, we are aware that her friends would be willing to cockblock if they felt the need. By befriending the group you could show genuine worry as to "where their friend was," especially as you saw the guy earlier flirting with another girl and getting pretty friendly with her in the quiet area at the back of the bar where he just took her friend.

As mentioned earlier these aren't techniques to be used lightly. They are deliberate and cutting, designed to ensure that the goal is achieved based on the bigger picture and definitely not to be used on a wing or anyone you care about. However using them on a natural is most definitely recommended. Remember, most guys that go out to a bar and chat to girls are trying to pull. They may not have the same knowledge of game as us and therefore the Metagame is even more deadly as they won't understand what is going wrong.

You can modify your game by using your knowledge of attraction and social interactions to achieve your goal whereas they will be left floundering. Even other PUA's who do not understand or use the Metagame will struggle to understand what is going wrong with their sets.

Let's take something as simple as opening:

In a particular venue, if you are aware that a guy is opening a large number of sets to build social proof, you can tailor your game and opening to use that as a means to hook the set. Simply wait for the guy to leave the set and move onto the next one, then move straight into the set he was previously in and open with a simple observational statement.

"Hey did you see that guy that just spoke to you? He's going around chatting to every girl in the room. Weird, eh?"

You can then sit with them and watch his behaviour with the girls, maybe even using your knowledge of game to explain what is going on. They are likely to be completely fascinated with the whole process of attraction, especially if you tell them when he is about to get blown out or eject before he does.

Using knowledge of game to talk to girls is something a lot of people would completely avoid for fear of appearing weird or giving the game away. However, most girls spend a lot of time reading about attraction and relationships in magazines. It's likely to be one of their favourite topics and something you are likely to have a lot of knowledge about. By telling them you have a healthy interest in social behaviour and read up on it in your spare time, you will have more than enough justification to speak to them about attraction. Also if someone opens them while you are in set, you can have an in joke with the girls as to their behaviour. Again, you can use the Metagame to alter the chances of the other guy.

Essentially the Metagame is fluid. It is used to adapt to every situation presented to you, utilising the information you have at your disposal and looking at the bigger picture to help achieve your goal. In fact, with solid Metagame, you should find yourself flourishing in male-rich environments as the only guy that stands out, even if they are all PUAs. While 20 guys will be approaching with opinion openers, you'll be approaching asking why people are going around asking for everyone else's opinion.

If used correctly you should be able to ensure that you can tailor your Metagame to deal with a variety of situations where normal game would struggle and help you stand out in a crowd of naturals and PUA's.

Re: Wise words from AMOG Scott: August 19, 2007

Girl turns up for day 2 and she is 30 minutes late.

AMOG Scott: You're dumped

HB: But there was a train delay!

AMOG Scott: You're still dumped. It doesn't matter how hot you think you are, leave earlier.

Next Scenario: AMOG Scott flirting with one of my wings girlfriends.

AFC AdamLondon: Hey dude, that girl you're chatting to is my friend's girl.

AMOG Scott: Why are you telling me that?

AFC AdamLondon: Because you're flirting with her.

AMOG Scott: Hey man, don't tell me. Tell her, she's flirting with me.

AFC AdamLondon: ...Erm.. OK... Good point... hahahaha... Seriously though, leave her alone.

AMOG Scott: OK, but if she follows me that's her problem.

Then my world fell apart...

AFC AdamLondon - I'm the Juggernaut Bitch (apologies in advance): August 20, 2007

Learn from this what you can about state building.

The following has been written following a break up with a girl I thought was particularly special. It's a long distance relationship but the distance has grown too much for us and a few days ago I started noticing her being a little more distant.

My posts are typically humble, calm, and something I hope you can all learn from. I write this at 4:25 a.m. and I promise you, if I met any girl right now I would fully close her. If I could demo, I would. This post is nothing like my normal posts. Instead I am letting my subconscious take over to give you an idea of how I am in state.

So I speak to the girl. It's a long ass conversation. I tell her she's grown distant, point out that she is struggling with the distance and that she isn't strong enough to make it work and tell her that it's OK. I wouldn't expect her to do anything that was too hard for her, that I'm still coming to see her and am going to ravage her. She's more than happy for the sexual reference.

Now my head. I cared about her. I cared about her a lot. Thankfully I'm no chode

On the phone I am anything but needy. She accuses me of having too much ego as I tell her of how much damage I'm gonna do in the States when I visit. She tells me I'm not that cool and I respond that Game + English Accent + USA = pussy.

(She doesn't know I've already contacted all 10 entourage girls that live in the States and invited them out on the weekend. Social proof, baby.)

She starts saying how excited she is that I'm going out there but by now the Juggernaut Bitch is ringing in my ears. She tells me she's going to hang up because I'm being too egotistical. I laugh and tell her she's more than capable of doing it if she wishes but that I still need to plan my sex with her and how I'm going to tease her in bed until she is begging to cum.

My state is pumping. It's 4:30 in the morning and I can't sleep. My heart is rushing in my ears. I could approach anything on the planet. I'd know exactly what to say and escalate so fast they'd be in my bed within moments.

I am not the man with whom to fuck. Those top PUAs have this mindset. It's there. Maybe below the surface like with me, but it's there for everyone.

I've been accused of having a very indirect style, which is only because I prefer to use it as I can game multiple girls at once that way. Though the direct style is always there to be used when necessary. Right now it's the only way.

I promised a friend that if it didn't work out with this girl, I'd hit the game with a vengeance. And I promise you all I shall. That doesn't mean books or articles, it means practice. My shit's tight right now, real tight. Though it's gonna get tighter. Really fucking tight.

Tyler says the aim in game is to get to a point where in a venue you know everyone and can open sets easily from warm approaches. Well London is about to become my venue, straight after I smash Dallas this week.

I love this community. A year ago I would have cried or been heartbroken over a break up. Now I'm infused with energy, knowledge, and game.

My friends and wings think I'm angry over the break up, though they are confusing anger with a high state and disappointment. I was hoping she'd be something special. She didn't have what it takes to have me.

This is the essence of higher value.

I don't feel I didn't close her, nor do I feel I did anything wrong. She didn't deserve me, and isn't right for me.

I get enough hot chicks not to care.

This is a game. Those who chose to participate are players like me. Those who stand back and watch whilst reading the articles are spectators.

Which are you?

AFC AdamLondon - women want me, men want to be me.

I didn't have much time to game as I had to meet the girl in Dallas. Whilst there I wrote this.

We need to make a conscious choice to improve: August 26, 2007

I've hit the game with a vengeance.

I hope you enjoy!

Why do we have a problem with forming relationships with others?

No matter how much you may try to tell yourself otherwise, we are here on this planet for one reason: to breed and survive. There may be other spiritual, political or even minor family reasons, however none of these would be possible if we didn't

replicate. It is no coincidence that two of the main four industries on the Internet include the porn industry and dating sites. Social networking sites making up one of the other two. This is our nature and the core of our very being.

You would think that we would be pretty adept at the one thing we were designed to perform. Unfortunately, this is not always the case. So many of us are actually incredibly unhappy with our marital status or current relationships. One of the main reasons is that we have no idea how we become attracted to others or why we end up in relationships. They are things that just happen.

You must have lost count of the amount of times that you have heard a guy friend of yours referring to getting a girl as *getting lucky* or a girl complaining that she only ever seems to attract losers. Is this really a coincidence? Are relationships really things that just happen to us, something that we have no control over? Or is there something more to this mystery?

By relationships we are talking about all forms; from marriage, to casual dating to one night stands. Believe it or not, all sexual relationships (I use the term sexual to differentiate between friends or peer groups) or interpersonal attractions are formed in a similar way, and follow a similar format.

This is a giant puzzle that hundreds of psychologists and scientists have been putting together for hundreds of years. In fact, far from being something that just happens, dating, attraction and sexual relationships follow a distinct pattern. It is one that can be learnt and one that can be reproduced.

A word of caution here: interpersonal attraction is not a hard skill. This means it isn't something that can be learnt through rigorous study and following a set of protocols. It is a soft skill, similar to art or football. It has a set of guidelines that help it along its course. Some people are naturally good while others need to be shown the theories. The fact is, no matter where you come from the more you practice the better you get.

Surely attraction is based on looks right? Wrong!

Just look back over the previous time periods and you will see that media images of what is perceived as attractive has changed dramatically over the last 50 years. It has gone from stick thin to voluptuous, lean to muscular. The fact is that what is seen as physically attractive depends on current trends and varies far too often to be a key trigger in finding someone to have a relationship with.

This is an example of comfort being reached straight away through propinquity as others are more willing to accept the potential partner based on their style or looks which match current social or media trends

Have humans always had a problem with this? The answer isn't so clear, however it's probably fair to assume that with our more hectic lifestyles and focus on material gain and work we have lost track of the correct way to attract a mate. Many people try to bribe others into a relationship with presents and promise of an even more materialistic lifestyle. Many of us have had some form of heartache in the past or situation that has caused us to fear either approaching someone we like, forming a relationship, or getting trapped in a cycle of being used by others. These issues cause us to view relationships differently and can get us caught in a repetitive cycle that is hard to break out of.

There is a reason we can be so general about these cycles yet know it applies to so many people reading this. That is because of the nature of learning in relationships. If you touched a fire you would burn your hand, thus a valuable lesson is learnt. Touching fire equals pain. Relationships aren't so easy. Most of us are kind enough to not want to hurt others feelings so when someone does something wrong we won't always tell them what went wrong straight away. This way we believe we are

protecting them from pain. Unfortunately all we are doing is removing the cause and effect line that would cause someone to learn from their mistake and be able to rectify it. Thus we end up repeating the same mistake over and over again.

Imagine touching a fire only to feel the pain two weeks later. Chances are we would forget the original reason for the pain and instead make an association between the pain and something else. So what we need is an outside intervention to break the cycle; a way to take a look at our situation and add external information.

This is why the game works.

AFC AdamLondon

....

Adding Value to build Comfort: August 26, 2007

When speaking to anyone new one of the key facts to consider is whether you are going to add value to them or take value from them. People are subconsciously aware of many factors relating to their interactions with others. If a homeless person were to initiate a conversation with you, you may instantly recoil from it without giving them time to speak. This is because you have a fear that they are likely to take value from you, either by asking for money or purely by association. If that homeless person were to suddenly begin the conversation by explaining that they were actually a secret spy in disguise, you would be much more likely to give them the time of day.

This is due to the fact that your perception of their value has changed; suddenly they are offering more to the interaction and giving you a cause to listen further. There are a number of ways to add value. The easiest is to quickly move the conversation onto an interesting topic right after the initial introduction. If you can't think of an interesting topic of conversation just remember that people love talking about themselves.

A WORD OF WARNING! -

Although people may enjoy talking about themselves, they seldom enjoy spilling out standard conversation about what they do for a living or how many sisters they have. This is simple conversation they have about 100 times a day as they meet new people. People prefer to talk about aims, ambitions and their joys in life. Deep questions about topics beyond the mundane are likely to yield much stronger results than basic conversation about their day-to-day drudgery.

Obviously there are a number of ways to add value and this isn't the only way to begin a conversation. If you have enough value already then the act of opening can often be the added value, as in a social proof situation. This is where it is apparent to everyone that you have the value so being in the conversation is the added value. This is a key element in direct game. The value may be from your aesthetics, social proof, or another element, but with that in place adding value is a piece of cake.

When you have the initial comfort the rest is easier.

Spot the guy who's writing far too much at the moment.

AFC AdamLondon

....

Number 1 PUA in the UK

World PUA Summit 2007 in Hollywood - The Forum Gets an Award! August 27, 2007

Heya Guys,

I have mentioned this a bit but thought I'd give ya'll a bit of a breakdown. I haven't been posting much over the last few weeks as I'm currently in the U.S of A!

Woo hoo!

I was invited to come out here and give a talk on some ideas I have about game at the world PUA Summit. Plus, with my girl being in Dallas I thought I'd kill two birds with one stone. They held the first PUA awards and our forum got the award for the largest community in the world!

How awesome is that? With all the discussions and arguments, we are the most active and largest in the world!

I accepted the award on behalf of the forum along with another award for myself as the number 1 PUA in the UK, which I don't know if I agree with so I made them add biggest AFC. I'm bringing the trophy home with me when I come back. The awards were televised and had a few members of Hollywood press present, although it was still a very small affair considering.

The summit rocked, there were loads of great people. I got to talk with Thundercat, Swinggcat and a whole bunch of other people who I'm sure I should have known, but didn't as I try to stay away from theory as much as possible. Channel 4 followed me the ENTIRE time! That was an absolute pain in the ass. You have no idea how annoying it is. I was trying to fix things with my girl, only to have them filming us from across the room trying to hear what we where saying.

Still, all in all, the whole thing was absolutely amazing and well worth the hassle.

Here's the best bit.

AFC: Adam, do you have any products for sale?

AFC AdamLondon: No

AFC: Do you run bootcamps?

AFC AdamLondon: No

AFC: Oh, so how do you teach?

AFC AdamLondon: I do the odd one-to-one and do free things as often as possible.

AFC: I don't get it.

AFC AdamLondon: Me neither, but I like making the community cheap!

AFC: Would you run bootcamps in the US?

AFC AdamLondon: Nah, I help my dad as a janitor in the evenings. Besides, I prefer London weather.

I was interviewed and asked the difference between game in the US and the UK.

I said, "Look around you at all the hats, sticks and goggles. In the UK, this would be a comic book convention. We prefer to be as NORMAL as possible advocating being social, and having fun, over using lines and tricks."

Anyway, I don't have much time to write but just wanted to say I miss you all very much, I love you guys, and that we rock the world!!!!!!!

AFC AdamLondon

p.s. Game is a piece of piss out here.

AFC AdamLondon: Hello.

HB: Wow, you're from England? Have you seen any of the clubs here? What about restaurants? ...Call me?

Sooo easy.

I didn't know how to feel. I'd been recognised as the Best PUA in the UK. It was scary and yet somehow rewarding. Though I hadn't sorted things out with the girl in the US properly, we were still kind of seeing each other.

I decided to add some FR's that I hadn't posted up previously to give a full breakdown of my system.

LR AFC AdamLondon using the framework: September 06, 2007, 05:07:08 PM

Hey guys. So, as promised, here's the LR I've been using as my own framework for a while now. It's easier (for me at least) if I can visualise what's going on.

I'm at Entourage. It's a one-off party and I'm alone with ten girls. Horrid situation eh?

Then a 2 set arrive, they are friends of Jim Stark. He's called the brunette, so she's out of the picture.

I pretty much vibe with the whole group, playing around and having fun. I'm building pre-selection and higher value. These qualities stack towards my qualities of attraction plus my cool, funky new hair and dress sense. The more of these qualities I have the more IOIs I receive. It's stupidly obvious really.

I get IOIs off of all the girls, though some more than others. I chat to all of them in turn to see which one I get on with. There's a really hot brunette who I number close before she has to leave with a friend. I didn't get enough time to chat to her but will day-2 at some point in the future. As luck would have it, the one I like the best is Jim's girl. Ha, sod's law. Another blonde is getting all over me and despite being incredibly hot is also incredibly drunk, so I'm not interested. Too many IOI's, too easy, too drunk.

However, Jim's girlfriend is actually not hanging out with us, she has moved onto another table as she fancies a guy on the table. Now that's a challenge I like.

I open her with, "what're you doing?" She tells me she fancies a dude and I confirm he's hot and that she should go for him. Have you guys read my Metagame stuff? If so you'll know that I've basically made him too available and killed the challenge.

Anyway, I tell her I'm going to show her something cool and move her to the interactive bar. We check it out for a bit and I think to myself, do I have comfort? Yes I do.

So I break rapport.

AFC AdamLondon: You know what? I'm kind of a blunt person. I find life easier that way, don't you?

HBTarget: What do you mean?

AFC AdamLondon: Well I can't be bothered to deal with people's crap. There are too many people that lie and talk rubbish and I'm not down with that. If I like a girl I tell her she is someone I fancy, that she looks hot, I like her and may want to have a few good meals and some great sex but that doesn't mean relationship. I mean, why would anyone want to do that? Why get into a relationship with someone you have only just met?

HBTarget: I know what you mean.

By being overly sexual I'm breaking the comfortable friend vibe we are having. I could probably have done it by picking on her or telling her we're in a fight, but I prefer sexual.

Then with rapport being broken I move on to attraction and qualification.

AFC AdamLondon: I hate crap sex too. Do you like crap sex?

(Qualifier)

HBTarget: No way.

AFC AdamLondon: Great sex is so much better isn't it?

HBtarget: Yeah, definitely.

So I broke rapport and she seems to be building it with me now... OK, what's next? I could continue to qualify just to make sure. If it goes wrong I can always revert to comfort and try again... however, I'm in my framework so why not follow it to the letter?

Sexual escalation.

AFC AdamLondon: You know, like when you really tease someone and trace a line up their leg with your tongue in between their legs while pinning them down and rubbing their back... There is something so great about the way the female body reacts to having her erogenous zones touched.

HBTarget: Yes.

AFC AdamLondon: (Leans in to her ear) Especially when you really tease someone (kiss her neck, leans out and looks into her eyes)

HBTarget: OMG yes... Wow, I'm so horny.

I lean back let things calm down. I don't know why really. I could have gone for the k-close then. But still, it doesn't matter.

She says she needs the toilet and I let her go. She comes back. Her body language has changed.

Her ASD is running high and she is looking to back away.

I laugh...it's back to the framework. I start with comfort again.

AFC AdamLondon: You're cute, you know that?

HBTarget: Why?

AFC AdamLondon: You have a cute little innocent face, which looks good yet hides a smile that says, "Wow, I really shouldn't have let myself get so turned on with someone I barely know in a night club." (Rapport break)

HBTarget: Yes.

AFC AdamLondon: I was thinking the same thing. (Comfort) I had the same feeling, but it felt good, didn't it?

HBTarget: Yes (Qualifying herself... attraction is in place and therefore assumed. Straight back to sexual escalation)

AFC AdamLondon: (leans in, moves hair out of face) It's just that I can't help it, I love teasing people and watching them squirm. I think you would look good rolling around arching your back as I tease you.

HBTarget: Mmmm

AFC AdamLondon: Let's go somewhere quieter

HBTarget: Where?

AFC AdamLondon: My flat

HBTarget: I don't think so. I'm not going to sleep with you.

AFC AdamLondon: Look, its not like we're going to have sex (nothing *like* it... we *are* going to have sex) **comfort**

AFC AdamLondon: I am going to tease you a lot. **break rapport**

AFC AdamLondon: So do you think you can handle it? **attraction**

HBTarget: Yes

AFC AdamLondon: Let's go then. **escalation**

Scary how obvious it is, eh?

She sends her friend home in a cab and we head to mine. I build comfort on the way. Play with breaking rapport, tell her she has a cute bum, get into the flat.

We start kissing and walk into the bedroom.

I fulfill the promise of teasing her, kissing her all over, getting her wet. We kiss some more, tease some more and it is purely sexual by now. I tell her what I'm going to do to her. There is no LMR whatsoever. We were only talking for one hour – why? Because she was horny and I have no expectations from her.

We kiss and I tease her to get her to the edge of orgasm. I tell her I won't let her cum, bring her back up and down.

HBTarget: Get a condom.

Game over.

AFC AdamLondon

FR Day game set - Park - Gym - AFCAdamLondon: September 12, 2007

Hey guys,

So as you all know I've been working on consolidating my game and getting it as good as I can, including ironing out the little glitches in my explanation of the formula I have developed for attraction.

So I've done some day sets. As I haven't posted a day game FR for a while I thought I'd add it in.

Set 1

I'm sitting in the park with two friends and I spot a cute dark haired girl reading a book. She pulls out a pen and begins writing on the book.

I take a quick second to calibrate. She has to be a student.

I open.

AFC AdamLondon: I'm sorry to bother you but I had to satisfy my curiosity. Are you a student? (Comfort)

HBItalian: Yep, I'm studying English.

AFC AdamLondon: And doing very well at it by the looks of things. At least a lot better than my Italian.

HBItalian: Really?

AFC AdamLondon: Yep, bella regazi (no idea if I spelled this wrong).

HBItalian: Thank you.

AFC AdamLondon: What for? (breaking rapport)

HBItalian: For the kind words.

AFC AdamLondon: Oh, I have no idea what I said. A friend told me to say it along with bella coulo (rapport broken).

HBItalian: OH! Your friend is a lot of trouble. It means nice lady and the other phrase is nice bottom.

AFC AdamLondon: Hahahaha funny, typical of her.

HBItalian: So are you from England?

AFC AdamLondon: Yep, born and raised. London in fact. I've always wanted to go to Venice. Where are you from?

HBItalian: Italy, you know where that is?

AFC AdamLondon: Of course! Hey, me and my friends are just hanging out in the park, do you have friends? (qualifier - attraction building)

HBItalian: Most of them are back in Italy.

AFC AdamLondon: Come and join us (leading and assuming attraction mixed with displaying lack of interest, all attraction building).

HBItalian: OK.

She then came and hung out with us for about 3 hours. During that time we had a piggy back race, ate food, she watched us play fight and I threw grass over her and threatened to attack her next.

Then we left the park.

I grabbed her by the waist and we walked off together arm in arm. As we left the park we kissed on the cheeks. I kissed her forehead (escalation) and we arranged to meet up again later this week.

Set 2

I'm in the gym working on my body. After the gym I treat myself to a trip in the mixed sauna. There is only one other person in there; a hot brunette with a tight body.

The scene: AFC AdamLondon, a sauna, a hot girl... it hardly seems fair, does it?

She starts singing. OMG, Why not just jump on the floor and spread your legs for me!

I sit listening, puzzling over whether I should open or just enjoy the beauty of her singing and perving over her. After all, once I open she'll be less attractive (my new thoughts about girls).

AFC AdamLondon: The first song was *Amazing Grace*, but I'm afraid I couldn't work out the second one (break rapport... I already had comfort as she was giving me an IOI by singing).

HBRussia: OMG, I'm so embarrassed. You could hear me?

AFC AdamLondon: (No, I'm deaf and can't hear things in a small wooden room) Yes I could. It reminded me of my mother who used to sing to me as a child, she was from the Ukraine (I heard the Russian accent - build a bit of comfort)

HBRussia: OMG, I'm from Russia!

AFC AdamLondon: No way! Awesome.

HBRussia: Yeah, so what were you doing here?

AFC AdamLondon: I was working out... at the gym.

HBRussia: So what do you do?

AFC AdamLondon: A lot of things. I believe it's important to live each moment as if it's your last. Too many people waste their time and then regret it later, I'm not one of those people.

We fluff for a while. Now I do a serious break in rapport.

After some particularly qualifying statements I tell her I'm heading to the jacuzzi and I'll see her around.

I wait 10 minutes then meet up with her in the lounge area. I knew she couldn't leave as she'd have to walk past me.

AFC AdamLondon: Following me, eh?

We talk a while longer and I tell her I have to leave but that I'd like to take her up on the offer of taking me to the Rose Garden Cafe (she didn't offer, but did tell me about it).

I tell her I don't have a pen to take her number and I ask her how much longer she will be at the gym

HBRussia: Well I've only just arrived.

AFC AdamLondon: Well how about I go get changed and meet you in the reception in ten minutes. You can give me your number then?

HBRussia: Yes, that works.

Hahaha! Seriously, she had just arrived and now has to get dressed to come outside to give me her number to go back again.

We swop numbers and I ask which direction she's heading in. She says:

HBRussia: Oh I'm going back into the gym to work out.

Hope this helps guys.

As always, if there are any questions just ask away!

AFC AdamLondon

Re: Wise words from AMOG Scott: September 20, 2007

AMOG Scott: She wasn't that bad looking, she just needed to

wear a shorter skirt.

hahahahaha

AFC AdamLondon

And obviously I was adding more advice as and when I worked them out.

I'm a bad man - leaving them better than you found them: September 24, 2007

Hey guys,

As you know, it's better to leave people in a better state than when you found them. Easier said than done right? I always quote my favourite theorist, Mr. Peter Parker. "With great power comes great responsibility"

How can we leave girls feeling better about themselves if we use them for sex? Well it all comes down to a question of telling the truth. You aren't using someone if they know the score from the beginning. It may come as a shock to many of you, however; GIRLS LIKE SEX.

Scary, but true. They just don't want to get lied to.

So here's a little something I say to girls to let them know I'm not looking for a relationship. You need to say it and genuinely be willing to walk away without her. I find that 90% of the time the girl will stay interested and you'll sleep with her anyway. They may not like it, they may not agree. They will appreciate the honesty and if you have sufficient attraction you'll probably still get the lay.

The following text was sent in response to the statements below.

AFC AdamLondon: I'm bad.

HB: You can't be *that* bad. Explain.

AFC AdamLondon: I'm simple really. I'm not really a relationship kind of guy. I don't offer anything beyond good fun, some nights out and occasionally great sex. If you can't handle that then I'm not the guy to talk to, you're better off finding someone else. I don't bullshit, I tell it as it is.

Hope this helps.

AFC AdamLondon

Theories to discuss... gaming without adding value: September 24, 2007

Hey guys, here's a question for you to think about.

Is it possible to game a girl without adding value? Like can you take someone to bed without displaying any form of DHV?

Are there other forms of DHV beyond wealth, violence - (think AMOG, natural types), knowledge?

I'm starting to believe that there may not be.

AFC AdamLondon

An approach to approach anxiety: October 10, 2007

Heya Guys,

I wrote this up too late to use on anything I've been working on and wasn't sure what to do with it. I just found it on my computer and thought I'd post it up.

Are you afraid of approaching someone you like through a fear of rejection?

Do you get that horrible feeling in your stomach and begin to formulate a hundred reasons why they wouldn't want to talk to you?

This is a lot more common than you would believe. There are a number of different products out there that will supposedly "fix" the fear of approaching strangers especially ones you are attracted to. However, few of them take the time to understand why we have that fear in the first place. If you understand why you have this fear or anxiety you can take steps to counter it. This is probably the biggest topic when it comes to understanding attraction. Well that is to say it is the one that most people have the biggest problem with. I constantly receive the same comments time and time again when it comes to this subject.

1) I'm scared of approaching.

2) I have a fear of rejection.

3) They aren't in the mood to be spoken to.

4) She won't think I look good enough.

5) I can't meet people in a park/cinema/night club.

6) I'm not good enough for him/her.

7) There's no point, it won't work.

These are probably the most common reasons I am given as to why someone can't approach, or the feeling that is preventing them from approaching. The fact that these are so prevalent is because they are all based on very real psychological factors to do with learning and behaviour.

Anxiety, as defined by Seligman, Walker and Rosenhan (2001), is a physiological state characterized by cognitive, somatic, emotional, and behavioural components. These factors essentially make up the feelings that we experience as fear, apprehension, and worry.

There are some physical sensations that you will probably be aware of such as **heart palpitations, nausea, chest pain, shortness of breath, sweaty palms**, shaking and perhaps headaches. These may be common to you. Some people will disguise these by making a **decision not to approach**, this will relieve the sensations and instead leave a sort of "numbness" to the situation.

Sigmund Freud himself believed that these anxious feelings were created by an association between a past negative experience and the current situation. These associations are often false and not related through causality - the idea that one situation directly affects another, but through correlation - one thing "tends to affect another over repeated attempts".

When people begin to see this correlation as a fact, it is commonly referred to as **"Magical thinking"**.

There are two governing principles behind magical thinking. The first is the law of similarity. The notion that things that resemble each other are casually connected in some way that defies scientific testing.

For example:

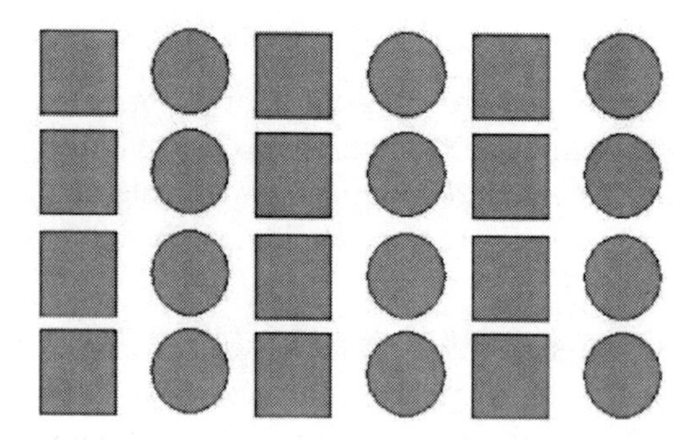

Here people will typically see vertical columns of squares and circles as opposed to horizontal mixed rows of squares and circles.

The second law is the *Law of Contagion*, which is the belief that "things that have been in physical contact or in spatial or temporal association with other things retain a connection after they are separated." Contagion effects have been noted to be more effective with negative associations than with positive ones. This is probably best explained by the notion of getting "bad luck" or having a bad time every time you go to a specific venue.

Freud believed that the anxiety or fear was maintained through a form of operant conditioning. Essentially the feeling of anxiety is reinforced everytime you are in a similar situation. You then "learn" to remove the negative feeling of anxiety by not approaching. These connections of patterns or "magical thinking" are common throughout all the human societies across the world. The human brain is adept at forming these patterns, though we do not have a particularly good system for distinguishing between real and perceived connections. Theoretically this is due to a simple survival tactic. If we notice rustling behind a bush it is better for us to assume it is some form of threat and begin to prep our bodies to defend ourselves, rather than ignore it and risk being eaten.

Our fear or anxiety response is actually designed to help us survive in a fight or flight scenario. Believe it or not, the symptoms detailed earlier are all beneficial to us in times of survival. Perspiration occurs to help cool us down, heart rate increases to improve blood circulation, muscles tighten as they are filled with oxygen in preparation for use. Unfortunately these are not particularly beneficial when we are looking for something witty to say during a conversation with someone.

In short **we learn the fear through a number of negative experiences** and then reinforce them by not doing anything about it. The body's natural reaction towards a fearful situation is the feeling we associate with approach anxiety or the fear of the approach. The way to overcome this is to reverse the learning.

All of the common problems detailed above can be directly related to either “magical thinking” in the form of a false belief that failure is almost certain due to some form of connection to a previous situation that failed or pure fear learnt and reinforced by not approaching. These are both forms of self fulfilled prophecy. Unless you actively do something to fix it they will continue to support themselves. The good news is that this problem is far from unfixable.

The bad news is that it does take time. The easiest way to fix this is to actually go out and meet new people. The problem is that when you do this, any negative experience you receive is likely to reinforce the previous attitude or fear you had before. As I’ve mentioned before one of the easiest ways to get around this is to simply meet people for the sake of meeting people.

Most of us are actually more than happy to talk to other people, especially on boring long journeys or when waiting in a long queue. Get used to talking to absolutely everybody, male or female, young and old. This should help you generate a great deal of positive responses to your approaches and help curb some of those negative connections.

I hope this helps guys. As usual, if there are any questions, just ask.

AFC AdamLondon

Un-Secret: October 16, 2007

I was teaching a student today and something clicked. Something big.

We were talking about opening sets and I suggested going into HMV to talk to girls about the DVDs they were buying just to get practice talking.

He then said something which I’ve heard many times before.

"I'm not interested in the DVDs they're looking at though"

Then it hit me. I am.

The difference between me and this guy was that I am genuinely interested in other people. The DVDs they buy, the clothes they want, making fun of them, making them laugh. These are all things that interest me. I have no problem approaching because my fear of approach is less than my desire to interact with someone.

My students fear is higher than his desire to interact with the girls, purely because he has little desire to actually talk to this girl. Yes, he wants to fuck her, but no he doesn't want to interact with her.

Think about it. Would you want to spend anytime whatsoever with someone who showed no interest in you?

I tested it further. I asked him if he would rather go to HMV and talk to girls about DVDs or play video games in doors. Guess what his answer was. He really did favour the latter. Though he felt he "should" speak to the girl as he does want to improve.

In his own words he felt sarging was akin to doing coursework. It was something he "had" to do. The problem is that when viewed like that you will get bad results. You'll be stuck in the game forever, never improving and wondering why.

In many ways it's the secret in reverse. If you don't want it, you wont get it. So I probed further.

AFC AdamLondon: Have you ever enjoyed sarging? Was there any time where it was fun?

Student: Yeah one time I went to some night club where people swap clothes for fun. Swaperama I believe it's called.

At this point I realised we could use that to duplicate the situation to make it as fun as possible.

We headed to Topshop. Warning: Routines below.

I told him to hold a dress up from the counter and ask, "Is this dress my colour?" Still he wouldn't open.

I asked him if he wanted to do it. Again, when we probed it came clear he didn't "want" to. He had fear but his desire was missing as well. The prospect of meeting new girls wasn't his true desire.

Then I remembered my first set ever. I was standing in Leicester Square with Catnap. We were to play kiss bandit which is where you run in front of a girl and tell her she can't pass till she kisses you. Of course this didn't work. Of course it was nuts. Yes, I looked like a dope. But I ran out to do it, to prove to myself that I could because I wanted to get better with girls.

It seemed crazy and pointless, but actually it wasn't. It made me confront my fear. It made me weigh up two factors. Fear vs Desire.

The one you want more is the one that will happen. My question to you is....

Do you really want to get good at this?

AFC AdamLondon

Then once again I found myself going to visit the girl in Dallas.

Vegas and Dallas: October 18, 2007

Heya guys!

I'm off to Vegas and then Dallas to do some talks on game.

Anyone got any cool ideas of where to go when I'm there? I've been to Dallas but haven't been to Vegas before and have no idea what's cool.

AFC AdamLondon

Love hurts: October 23, 2007

So I'm seeing this Texan girl. Hell! I'm in Texas at the moment.

I can't explain to you guys the extent of what has happened, but I will eventually. Right now I just have to vent. Game is great up to a point. The fact is, if I lived here she would be mine. I have no doubt, but I don't live here.

That doesn't change how I feel about her, but it does affect things. I just had the worst night of my life with relationships since joining game.

It is oneitis definitely. Love definitely.

The thing is, it has made me realise that I don't want random girls or fucks. I do just want a girlfriend. I want to get married, get old and die happy.

I miss you all.

Adam

Though understanding the game was not making things easier. In fact it was making things a lot harder.

We all had the dream of seeing the matrix and being like Neo, yet the truth was closer to that than we realised.

The Problem with Seeing Matrix: October 23, 2007, 03:52:28 PM

Can you spot IOI's?

Do you know how to escalate and convert almost every day 2 into a Lay?

Do you consider getting numbers the norm?

If so, you took the red pill and can see the matrix.

One of my good wings pointed something out to me recently and I can't believe how right he was.

Congratulations, you're in the matrix! Unfortunately we aren't all the Neo's we want to be.

There is a massive fucking issue with the Matrix. Instead of Neo, we're all Syler. You see when we see the matrix, we realise....We didn't fucking want it.

Honestly, the world was a safe place compared to the one full of robots. Who wants a real world when you can live in the relative bliss of ignorance?

Every girl we see we can get. We know how to get her into bed, we can take what we want, but then it loses it's value. That which we don't work for has no value for us. So we move on looking for the next best thing. Until we find her.

What about the one we can't get? Unfortunately, by definition, we can't get her.

So now we are straight back at square one: hunting for the girl we can't get. Only now it's that much harder because every time we get one we lose interest.

Sometimes... sometimes... I wish I could go back to the world where I had a girl who was *alright*. I'd be happy and content and not think about whether I could get anything better.

I'm getting older and as I age I want stability, a real relationship and marriage. The longer I'm in the game, the harder I believe it will be. Not finding a girl. But finding one I'm happy with.

AFC AdamLondon

....

Re: Social Proof Help Required - What to Read? November 18, 2007

The Mere Exposure Effect – This is the idea that merely sharing one or two warm interactions with someone will make them perceive you in a favourable light. More importantly, imagine walking around a room where you have shared these favourable experiences with a number of people in the venue. As you walk heads will be turning, people will be smiling at you as you walk around, others will be noticing it. Your propinquity will be increasing tenfold with every person you speak to as the mere exposure effect travels around the room.

Suddenly you will find yourself in a situation where absolutely everyone in the room is favourable towards you. There won't be anyone you can't speak to and, if done correctly, a whole bunch of people will be wondering exactly who you are. This can happen in absolutely any location; from a train or bus to a top celebrity night club in the best part of town.

There are a number of different techniques that will help you with this.

You can see how with this it would be easy to move around staff in a venue and vibe with them in a nice way, but what about people who aren't predisposed to be nice to you? In these situations it's important to learn the different ways to get new people to be friendly towards you.

First off, don't worry if you get a negative reaction. You're playing a bigger game. People around you are unlikely to notice you receiving a bad reaction, mostly due to the fact that many people are polite in the rebuttals. Just make sure that you leave any interaction in the most positive way possible.

A simple phrase such as;

"I'm so sorry to have upset you, I was only looking to have a conversation with someone new. I hope I haven't offended you. Have a great night."

Naturally you'd prefer to have a whole bunch of perfect interactions, but there is just no way of knowing whether a given interaction will always go well; obviously the more your mere exposure and propinquity built up, the better responses you will get. The trick is trying to make sure the earlier one's go as well as possible until you have the required level of social proof to be able to vibe with the entire room.

There are a number of different ways to begin speaking to people. Whatever you decide to use ultimately, there are two things to bear in mind. Try not to be threatening initially and try to add value to everyone you meet.

The first point is pretty self explanatory; after all, you're trying to have a number of positive interactions with those around you. The second point may not be so easy to understand. When you go out for a party or do your shopping you have a number of things planned in your head that you want to achieve. You do not want someone hassling you or preventing you from achieving those things. Essentially you are not looking for someone to interfere or lower the value of what you are doing.

Bare this in mind when speaking to new people. Value can be added in many ways, from adding fun and interesting conversation, to giving compliments, to just being the social hub of the party bringing that vibe to the people. Either way, remember that you're approaching them so try to be courteous, yet there's no harm in being fun and a bit flirtatious.

Remember, you don't initially want to spend too much time talking to the people, especially if you are likely to be around for a while, such as in a restaurant, coffee shop, long journey or a night club. Allow the first interaction to end quickly, ideally on a positive high note, then you can move on talk to a few other people, and then go back to them later for an even better reaction.

With that in mind here are a number of quick ways to get some conversations started;

"Does this train lead to [insert destination here]... Thanks so much for that I got on in such a rush I didn't bother checking."

"You know, that food looks great. It's definitely what I would have normally, though today I'm being brave. What should I try?"

"Is this the only dance floor here?"

"Does it ever get busier in here?"

"Wow, I love that jacket, it really works with the handbag and everything. I had to stop and tell you, it's rare to see someone accessorise so well."

"Why do crowds have to be so full of people? Wouldn't it be easier if this was just a private road? You could have that part, and I could have this bit."

These are all really simple ways of getting a small vibe going with the people around you. Then simply move around the area, having occasional conversations with people until eventually you have built up enough positive reactions that everyone in the room or area has been spoken to.

Then it is time to move back round and re-speak to the ones you want to actually have a conversation with and begin building some form of connection with them.

AFC AdamLondon

At this point, things with the girl in Dallas were getting interesting. She had booked a ticket to come and visit me for Christmas. However, I still needed to practice my game if only to keep my skills sharp. I figured I'd practice online. That way I wouldn't have to meet them in person.

FR: Online Facebook Chat AFC AdamLondon Text Game: December 18, 2007

Heya guys,

I've been using a slightly altered type of my own game to really bring girls into my life fully. There is no lying or hiding anything from them, just cool girls up for an open relationship. I can even talk to them about my other girls.

I've done this through a solid frame and massive qualification. All my wings know about this and I know Sugarpuss has used it, maybe even wrote an fr. However, I had cut and pasted this conversation to MrM to show him the results I'm getting and thought I'd send it up for ya'll too.

Hope it helps!

AFC AdamLondon

AFC Adam London: I've been working all weekend, non-stop before Xmas. Cashing in for presents! How bouts you?

There's loads I've always wanted to ask you but have shied away because you seem cool. I was always waiting till we met up but seeing as how most of our conversations are on Facebook, I reckon I may start them here.

HB: OK, ask away....

AFC AdamLondon: Well... You must have heard I'm a lot of trouble and yet you still flirt your cute little bum off with me. Why?

HB: Hmmm, that's a good one! Not the usual shit that everyone asks....

I'm not sure really, I suppose it's because when I'm out I don't usually meet many people that I can hold an enjoyable conversation with. Yet with you, we always find something to talk about, be it for 5 minutes or half hour. And no, I hadn't heard how much trouble you can be......

AFC AdamLondon: Hahaha, I don't believe in talking crap to people, I think it wastes everyone's time and ends up with people getting hurt. I hate hurting people, really not my style. I'd rather be blunt and open.

Have you heard what I actually do for a living? I was on a TV show last week, a Channel 4 documentary. I know a few people saw it, did you?

HB: No, I didn't know CH4 made a documentary about you, that it was on last week, or what it was about for that matter! Clueless about that one! Is that why you were away so much in America? You'll have to fill me in.

AFC AdamLondon: You must be the only person I know that doesn't know. It's weird because I know what you mean about always having conversation and I love your energy, the way you always bounce around so happy.

Oh man, this is funny. I've never had to explain all this to someone online before. Hahaha, well I'm regarded as a pretty good seducer. They followed me out to LA to collect an award. Essentially it's due to my style, which is that I don't believe in lying to people.

[Hey guys watch how I switch to describe what I say to girls yet it reads as if I'm saying it to her! I do this a lot.]

I meet a girl I like, and tell them that life is too short to just randomly jump into some committed weird relationship where you both end up hating each other. I like to really get to know a girl first, and I'm not going to cut out all my other friends for some chick I've only just met.

I'm a lot of trouble. You're either the kind of girl that can handle that, or you're the kind of girl looking for something more and hoping to change a bad-boy. I can't be changed.

If you're the other type then you need to stay away because you'll get hurt, so I'll just keep things friendly and at distance because I don't want to hurt you.

And then the girl gets to choose how she treats me. No lines or lying, just pure honesty. She likes me or not.

HB: OK, well I knew you had a dating school or something like that from the conversations we have had, but that was about it....

Your ethos is all very well and good at our tender young age, and in part I agree. But what about as you get older? Is this a lifestyle? Or just for the CH4 show? I always thought you were such a nice, polite, quiet person! Oh how I was wrong! hehe!

AFC AdamLondon: Hahaha, yeah you have no idea. I'm a hell of a lot of trouble, I just hide it well. It's something for this stage in my life. When I'm older I won't be able to keep up with the pace.

I also have strict rules about one night stands, in that I refuse to do them. I'd much rather spend time with a cool chick that I really get on with for a decent amount of time just with no strings. Besides the sex gets better the more you do it. ;o)

I figured I should warn you in advance because I really am a lot of trouble. But I have a fondness for you and your cute bum in particular.

HB: The more I hear about this, the better it sounds. So thanks for the advanced warning, but bring on the fun! Are you out on Wednesday? It's the Santa night! hehe

AFC AdamLondon: Hehehe I wasn't sure about going, but if you're going to be there, I may steal you into the R&B room for a quiet dance. ;o) I hope you aren't as timid and shy as you appear....

HB: Haha, you don't know what you've let yourself in for! xx

AFC AdamLondon: Hahaha, good answer, but right back at ya kiddo. I really do hope you are as feisty as you just hinted because I'm going to drive you wild. I hope you can handle being teased... ;o)

HB: I love it! You're in for a treat! x

AFC AdamLondon: You too.. ;o) X

Life had taken a crazy turn for me. The road to this point had been purely about improving my own game and learning the abilities to help me get the girl of my dreams. Shortly after this field report I was notified that the Thundercat Seduction Lair had voted me as the 3rd Best Pick Up Artist in the world! This was no light accolade. This same listing was the one which introduced Neil Strauss to the seduction community as a whole and helped him become recognised as a great PUA which, of course, he wrote about in his book *The Game.*

My name in the UK had risen as well. I had been covered in all of the national papers, a few of the mens magazines and demand for my teaching increased with every satisfied student. After years of thinking they would either never improve their skill or that they where restricted to only improving with the aid of peacocking props and negging as openers, people where finding better and better results only being themselves.

More and more students were coming to me for training as my name was pushed throughout the community. I was one of the only people to begin putting my exploits on film. Uploading these to YouTube became a way of me helping others duplicate my success without even having to meet me. Though with all the work and all the girls I was meeting something was missing. I didn't have a special someone in my life. The main reason I had joined the community wasn't just to get girls, it was to learn the ability to get a special girl. Someone who I could grow up with and enjoy life, smiling at the funny things we do each day and laughing at each other as our bodies fall apart.

Luckily fate would have it's hand in this.

I'd spent a lot of time with a French girl. She was a model for Storm Modeling Agency and she was different to the other girls. I wasn't interested in gaming her as such, rather I enjoyed spending time just hanging out and laughing. In between all of the field reports and posts you've been reading I would spend my time sitting with her and sharing the stories, teaching her the skills as I learnt them and generally just enjoying time. Every night when I left to go to a club I would invite her out for a date the next day, and every time I would stand her up.

I can't explain why fully. I just wanted to keep one girl away from myself. Let one girl in on my world telling her everything I do but keeping her safe from myself and my "game." Time disappeared and over a period of six months we spent more and more time together. I never kissed her because I was fearful of losing my respect for her as she became just another one of the girls.

Then it happened, she left.

Her modeling contract had run out and she was due to move back to France. On the last day before she left I offered to take her out to dinner to celebrate. This was never documented on a forum or as part of my diary. I suppose this was my way of still treating her differently to the others.

AFC Adam: Hey girl, so how about you and me do a final leaving dinner before you move to France forever. Heck, I'll have to come and visit you there as well just to continue our chats.

French girl: We need to talk

AFC Adam: What's wrong?

French girl: Why did we never hook up?

AFC Adam: I'm sorry? What do you mean?

French girl: Every day you come and talk to me, we shoot the rubbish about your life and the girls you sleep with yet you've never made a move on me. I've waited for ages for you to do something and you haven't ever gone for it. I don't understand why you don't like me. Still you've had your chance. I'm not waiting any longer. I'm off to France and you can play around with all your girls and enjoy your life alone.

AFC Adam: ...

With that she left. Not another word, just got up and walked away. I was devastated. I could have easily made a move and had her but doing this would have ruined the special position she had in my life. And apparently not making a move was equally as bad.

Here I was regarded as one of the top seduction and dating experts in the world, yet I was struggling to make myself happy when it truly counted. The random girls weren't fulfilling the void and I wasn't making a move on the special ones because of the other girls in my life.

With the loss of the French girl I knew I had to change something. The random encounters and girls hanging around weren't conducive to meeting the girl I wanted to be with. It was time to do something drastic. I wasn't going to let myself miss an opportunity like this again, to be with the person I wanted to.

I decided I would drop every single girl I was with the second I met a girl who was worth being with. As soon as I met someone who just gave me any indication that they might be worth changing my life for I would jump in head first and deal with the consequences later.

Within only a few short months I met a girl by the name of Amanda. She turned out to be completely different to any other girl I had ever met.

Though of course that is a completely different story...

This book is a collection of my own experiences and the journey I followed throughout my own development of my dating life. I went from being someone who would struggle to even talk to girls to someone who lived a life possibly only rivaled by Hugh Hefner yet realising that at the end of the journey all I really wanted was to find love.

This book wasn't designed to ever be read by anyone else. It's a mixture of diary entries, forum posts, and my own theories mixed in with a few paragraphs from myself to glue it all together. It isn't designed to be a great read or even a book worth noting, rather an insight into the life I lead for a while that ended up with me becoming known as one of the worlds top experts on seduction.

This journey is easy for you to follow. As you can tell it isn't without pain or hardship, and it takes a lot of time and dedication, but wherever you are now, you could be seeing incredible results within only a relatively short time if you work at it.

If you enjoyed reading this book and got even the smallest piece of advice from it, please pass it on. I hate the thought that somewhere out there a guy is sitting in his room playing video games alone thinking he will spend the rest of his life lonely and eventually die alone with no one to care for him. This thought drove me to be as good as I can be, and still drives me to help others.

Pass the knowledge forward and help those around you, so we can all find someone that loves us.

Adam Lyons

Glossary

AMOG: Alpha Male of Group/Alpha Male the Other Guy

BF: Boyfriend

BUYER'S REMORSE: A feeling of regret a woman may feel after becoming intimate with another person

CLOSE: The end result of an interaction. This may be taking the woman's phone number (number close), kissing the woman (k-close), or sleeping with her (f-close)

DAY 2: The second meeting. A third meeting would be Day 3 etc.

DHV: Demonstration of Higher Value

FR: Field Report. An account of an interaction with another woman, without f-closing [see above]

GAME: The process of developing a relationship with a woman. The setting in which this takes place usually precedes this word; e.g. street game would be meeting women on the street

HB: Hot babe

IOI: Indicator of Interest (i.e. a woman showing she likes you)

IN-FIELD: In an interaction with a woman or group of women

INNER GAME: One's attitude and mentality, this includes issues such as confidence

KINO: Touching

LJBF: Let's Just Be Friends

LMR: Last Minute Resistance;

LR: Lay Report. A field report but one which has ended with a f-close

LTR: A Long Term Relationship with a woman

MLTR: One of several Multiple Long Term Relationships

NEG: A backhanded compliment

ONEITIS: Developing a strong emotional attachment to one particular woman

OPENER: The first sentences you say to a woman or group of women

OUTER GAME: The forms of communication (e.g. verbal, body language) one use's to attract women

PUA: Pick-Up Artist; a person who practices the art of attracting and closing women

SARGE: Going out with the intention of picking-up women

SET: Group of girls (e.g 2-set is two women)

SOCIAL PROOF: Increasing your attractiveness within a set environment by being seen to know and talk to everyone, or getting attention from other women.

CPSIA information can be obtained at www.ICGtesting.com
Printed in the USA
BVOW012336020512

289320BV00010B/22/P